The Future of Reading

Why do we read? What happens to our imaginations when we read? To our knowledge? What creative forces are unleashed? What are the wider implications of all of this?

In a truly engaging and accessible style, *The Future of Reading* looks at the very *experience* of reading; not just the consumption and interpretation of texts, but also reading as an artistic process that demands creative freedom and unfolds from deep in the soul. Rather than analysing or critiquing texts, this book examines what happens to us when we read: the complex human experience which frees us from certain boundaries and constraints, and then looks at how we can use this freedom of mind to creatively tackle much larger issues in the world. Eric Purchase argues that creative reading enables us to generate answers for complex, real-world problems that cut across fields of knowledge and, therefore, defy solution by experts.

Enjoyable, challenging, unique, and astute, this book will open up the reading experience for students and all readers interested in using literature and reading as a positive force in their lives and the world.

Eric Purchase earned a PhD in Comparative Literature from the University of Connecticut, USA. He taught writing and literature there, and at other universities, for 12 years. He now works as a professional writer and an independent scholar.

The Future of Reading

Eric Purchase

Routledge
Taylor & Francis Group

LONDON AND NEW YORK

First published 2019
by Routledge
2 Park Square, Milton Park, Abingdon, Oxon OX14 4RN

and by Routledge
52 Vanderbilt Avenue, New York, NY 10017

Routledge is an imprint of the Taylor & Francis Group, an informa business

British Library Cataloguing-in-Publication Data
A catalogue record for this book is available from the British Library

Library of Congress Cataloging-in-Publication Data
Names: Purchase, Eric, author.
Title: The future of reading / Eric Purchase.
Description: Milton Park, Abingdon, Oxon; New York, NY:
Routledge, 2019. | Includes index.
Identifiers: LCCN 2018046785 | ISBN 9781138319493
(hardback: alk. paper) | ISBN 9781138319523 (pbk.: alk. paper) |
ISBN 9780429844041 (epub3) | ISBN 9780429844034 (mobipocket) |
ISBN 9780429453885 (master) | ISBN 9780429844058 (adobe reader)
Subjects: LCSH: Reading, Psychology of. | Books and
reading—Psychological aspects. | Literature—Psychology.
Classification: LCC BF456.R2 P87 2019 | DDC 153.6—dc23
LC record available at https://lccn.loc.gov/2018046785

ISBN: 978-1-138-31949-3 (hbk)
ISBN: 978-1-138-31952-3 (pbk)
ISBN: 978-0-429-45388-5 (ebk)

Typeset in Bembo
by codeMantra

To Paula

Contents

Preface

You never encountered a book like this before. If you've read something about reading or teachers have talked to you about it, they probably discussed what books to read, why reading is good for you, or how to read. These are the standard ways to frame the topic of reading. Thus, in *The Future of Reading*, you might expect to find appreciations of great books and authors, arguments about the role that reading plays in our society, and explanations of literary theory. But you will be disappointed.

Instead, this book describes the uses of reading. Books don't mean anything unless they make a difference in your life. You can use reading to solve the most complex problems you face as an individual and as a citizen. Think about reading, then, as a powerful tool and *The Future of Reading* as your owners manual.

I wrote the book following the same principles that I advocate in it for reading. I approached my task as a problem to solve, and I improvised a solution from the resources I had on hand, namely, my own experiences of reading. Therefore, the texts I discuss in *The Future of Reading* do not represent "the best which has been thought and said in the world." I don't claim my interpretations of them are the right ones. I don't advocate any of the ideas and political positions cited in the book. These texts and ideas serve only to illustrate my points about reading; they are useful for that specific purpose. Beyond that, I take no responsibility. Use them for your own purpose if you find them helpful. If not, discard them, and look for better texts and ideas elsewhere.

Don't allow the examples in the book to limit your imagination of what is possible with reading. The choice of texts in *The Future of Reading* reflects my own peculiar history. I studied literature in school, so most of the examples come from novels, poetry, and plays though

I include some from economics, psychology, religion, science, and other fields. The jumping off point for the book is literature, too, because the study of reading is generally assumed to belong in that department. Nevertheless, the pragmatic approach to reading I describe applies to any texts in any discipline. Whatever you have read will give you all the resources you need to get started.

Acknowledgements

The author would like to express his deepest appreciation for the generosity of those who read this work at various stages and provided valuable encouragement and suggestions for improvement: Brian Bennett, Jamie Carr, Guo Jian, Paula Kot, and Ross Miller. I would also like to thank Polly Dodson and Zoe Meyer of Routledge for their support as well as Jeanine Furino and Esther Saks of codeMantra.

Gwendolyn Brooks' poem, 'The Bean Eaters', has been reprinted with consent of Brooks permissions.

I acknowledge no fixed rules for the interpretation of the Word of God, since the Word of God, which teaches freedom in all other matters, must not be bound.

—Martin Luther

CHAPTER 1

The freedom of a reader

Have you ever said to yourself, "I'm not going to form an opinion about our Afghanistan strategy until I hear from the Poet Laureate?" Probably not. We view literature as a means of reflecting on the world rather than as a way to engage it directly.

When we consume literature, we make unspoken assumptions about the nature of reading. Reading is a cultural form that encourages and discourages certain behaviors. If we change the form, we enable different behaviors. We give ourselves new capabilities. We can acquire more power over our own lives and in the world at large by adopting new reading habits.

Unfortunately, we accept the form of reading that we learned at home and in school without a second thought, not realizing how it limits us. To create a new form, we must reconsider the fundamentals of reading, starting with the main elements: the writer, the text, and the reader. Typically, we imagine the page as a kind of rear-projection screen. The author sits out of sight behind the screen and projects words onto it. We readers sit in front of the screen. We can't see what the writer is doing. We merely consume the words as they appear before our eyes.

In this model, the writer plays an active role. He puts a great deal of thought and effort into creating the text. We admire this creativity. We allow him all freedom to develop it. The text comes from somewhere deep in the writer's soul. Its source is ultimately unknowable. The writer's uncommon skill and the inaccessibility of its source enhance the value of the text in our eyes.

By contrast, the reader is passive. We are supposed to take the text as a given. We do not question its integrity. We restrict ourselves to determining what the writer means. Or if we grant that the meaning extends beyond the author's intention, we look for what the text means. We employ theories and methods to ensure we come up with an interpretation that remains true to the text, uncontaminated by our personal concerns. We do not allow the reader an artistic process, comparable to the writer's, which demands creative freedom and unfolds from deep in the soul.

In short, we do not give the activity of reading enough respect. We do not distinguish reading clearly enough from the text. We study fiction, poetry, and plays in school because they are revered for their literary excellence. The term "literature" confounds what we read with the value we derive from it. We view the text and its value as nearly identical. We internalize the text in order to possess its value. We often satisfy our curiosity about a friend's reading by asking for the title as if knowing which book someone has read tells us all we need to know about the value he derives from it. This melding of text and value makes it hard to conceive of a form of reading that is not just a mirroring of the text in our mind or a set of methods and interpretations. Yet we know such a model is inaccurate. Suppose we both read the same book. It changes your life, but it bores me. We didn't merely interpret the text differently; we had radically different experiences of it. A lot more has gone on inside us than absorbing the text into our consciousness.

Reading is not merely an intellectual activity. It is a complex human experience, like the relationships, work, travel, health, and other circumstances that define our lives. Like them, reading can sustain our whole weight if we need it to. As with them, the feelings we experience when we read deserve minute observation. We can thereby turn reading into a deliberate pursuit. We can read more creatively and derive more value from the experience. And that value will be differentiated—uniquely mine, uniquely yours, fitted for where we are and what we need to do.

Creative reading enables us to imagine the world *as a whole* and to conjecture solutions for the problems we encounter in it.

This vision of reading can address "wicked problems," which consist of multiple, interlocking challenges. We can't solve Challenge A until we solve Challenge B. We can't solve Challenge B until we solve Challenge C. We can't solve Challenge C until we solve Challenge A.

Here's an example. Say we want to increase crop yields to feed a growing world population. The plant scientists create a genetically engineered version of corn that resists weed killer. The farmer can efficiently spread herbicide over all of his fields to kill the weeds without harming the corn, which then grows fatter from not having to compete for nutrients. The corporation for which the scientists work patents the genes. The patent gives the corporation the power to dictate that farmers must buy new seeds every year for the corn—they cannot retain seed corn for the next year as farmers have done for 10,000 years. The corporation audits the farmers every year to ensure compliance. Wind blows the pollen from the genetically modified corn into a neighboring field and pollinates the corn there. The corporation, therefore, sues that farmer to claim the fee for its intellectual property, which found its way there by chance. Farmers using ordinary seed corn cannot compete with the yields garnered by farmers who use the genetically modified version, so economics forces them to buy the new corn, too. The triumph of the new version threatens to create a monoculture. A staple crop for humans and animals has become more vulnerable to being wiped out by a disease or biological attack. Other countries view the genetically modified corn as a threat to their agriculture and possibly to human health, so it becomes a cause of trade friction and a subject of testing by medical researchers. Thus, the plant scientists who simply wanted to increase crop yields have triggered a series of consequences, most of which they did not foresee, in farming, economics, accounting, ethics, law, medicine, national security, and international trade. There is no simple solution. If we ban genetically modified corn, farmers will produce less, and possibly consumers somewhere in the world will have less food to eat. If we allow genetically modified corn, the structures and expectations around farming must be adjusted, often painfully.

We leave these kinds of questions for experts and formal institutions to answer. We feel such problems lie beyond the power of an ordinary person to solve. However, experts also lack an ability to address them because they overflow the watertight containers of knowledge through which they understand the world. Doctors, lawyers, professors, engineers, scientists, and other professionals gain their authority by acquiring deep knowledge in narrow fields. That is because we have constructed institutions and incentives to reward specialization. Experts solve problems beautifully within their own fields. They flounder when problems extend beyond them.

We continue to put our faith in rational inquiry and specialists to solve problems for us, and they keep failing us when we need solutions most urgently. The International Monetary Fund recommended austerity to countries during the 2008 financial crisis, based on economic principles, only to admit error after those countries suffered terrible job losses. But even when economists recognized their mistake and found the right solution—increased government spending—they could not persuade politicians to follow their advice.

Every member of the U.S. Supreme Court attended Harvard or Yale. They may be the most highly qualified jurists in the court's history. They have also divided along partisan lines, and the court has lost much of its reputation for impartiality.

Sophisticated medicine fumbles when it faces patients like my father whose disease cuts across medical specialties. The cardiologist knows little about bowel trouble, the gastroenterologist little about depression, the family physician little about blood disorders, and the hematologist little about heart conditions. So how will they diagnose a man who experiences symptoms in all four areas? He dies slowly while they search programmatically for an answer. After five fruit-less trips to the emergency room, I decided to do a little reading on my own. I reasoned that my father probably had a common ailment and soon identified heart failure. I reached this diagnosis before the doctors precisely because I have no medical training and, therefore, lack the conceptual categories and protocols that divide up this field of knowledge. Doctors will warn against the danger of laymen at-tempting a diagnosis. Yes, it is dangerous anytime we allow reading to have direct, real-world consequences. It is also dangerous to trust experts blindly. I still go to the doctor when I'm sick, but I ask a lot of questions.

We have to go back to antiquity to find an intellectual model for a universe not divided by specialized knowledge. The ancients embraced a more comprehensive vision of the world than we mod-erns see. In *The Nature of the Universe*, the Roman poet Lucretius argues that people should not succumb to the worries aroused by superstition and religion because the world is wholly physical and can be understood rationally. The book's famous invocation of Venus indicates how gracefully Lucretius melds the physical and the human realms:

> Mother of Aeneas's descendants, pleasure of humans and gods,
> nourishing Venus, who enjoys visiting, under gliding
> constellations, the ocean with its ships, the earth
> with its fruits. Through you the whole kingdom of animals
> is conceived and watches the sun's light rising up.
> You are the one, goddess, that the winds flee from; the clouds of
>   the sky
> flee before you and your coming; for you the sweet, beautiful earth
> sends up flowers; for you the surface of the sea laughs,
> and the calmed sky shines with spreading light.

(I, 1–9)

The elegance of these lines conceals a complex imagination of the world. The mythological figure of Venus is at once the planet Venus, sexual desire, and the mother of Aeneas, who founded the Roman people. Thus, the material objects of the universe, the human and animal instincts, and the historical and cultural context of Lucretius' readers become inextricable. The function of Venus as a divinity quietly disappears inside these three aspects. We do not need to assume that supernatural powers govern the world because the material ones that Venus represents calm the earth on their own in a predictable rhythm just as reason calms a mind beset with irrational fears. If we respond to the beauty of the verse—how can we resist?—we have already primed ourselves to accept Lucretius' philosophy before we have read ten lines.

Similarly, the physical, moral, and poetic arguments of Lucretius' work reinforce one another. Lucretius asserts that the universe consists of atoms moving through a void, a proposition not too different from the teachings of modern physics. Nevertheless, his universe never becomes the inhuman emptiness it does in our science. The very images that Lucretius uses to explain the universe keep it human. For instance, he demonstrates the atomic theory of matter through the example of a gold ring which becomes thinner after years on someone's finger. Invisible particles must have been wearing off the whole time. Atoms thereby become associated with a symbol of warmth and remembrance. He shows that the universe is infinite by asking us to imagine what would happen if the universe did have an outer limit: a warrior could run out to the boundary and hurl a spear over it. There must always be further space for the spear to fly into. This vignette reads like episodes from Roman military history where the centurions hurl battle standards over the palisade of the enemy's camp to spur the troops into storming it to retrieve the standards and the honor of the legion. In a wholly physical universe, the gods are unnecessary; the world progresses on its own through the movement of the atoms. This godless, materialistic, yet human-scale universe implies its own morality. The grand objects of life in society—god and country—mean nothing in a universe of innumerable atoms and infinite void. Therefore, according to Lucretius, the best people can do is maximize their personal happiness. The good life involves quiet, moderate enjoyment of friendships, study, and physical pleasures. We must not overdo anything, he warns, not become a slave of our own appetites once we have liberated ourselves from the illusion of religious and political duty.

Lucretius addressed a complex challenge of his time at the end of the Republic. Rome had acquired a vast empire. Many residents of Rome came from somewhere else. They brought their own gods and religions. Roman religious institutions started to seem less inevitable and sometimes a bit parochial, such as the college of 15 *haruspices*, who sacrificed a goose, examined its liver for portents of future events, and reported them to the government. Rome's official religion functioned as an extension of the state. Only the politically powerful and their associates could hold important priestly offices. Religious ceremonies and teachings reinforced the government. Getting ahead in this environment involved questionable activities: joining the army to accumulate booty from foreign conquests, becoming a government official to skim money off the top, or using connections with powerful people to start a business. Various factions at Rome vied for political power, and the winners had a habit of executing or exiling the vanquished. Success of any sort was fragile. This situation posed a number of questions: Where do you direct your energy if politics and self-dealing taint the conventional measures of success, such as military glory and wealth? What does a moral life consist of if the traditional Roman virtue of selfless dedication to the noble fatherland is no longer possible? How do you find meaning in life if you lose respect for the religious customs and institutions you grew up with? Today, one imagines that experts would tackle these problems separately—the theologians addressing the spiritual question, the political scientists addressing the political question, the psychologists addressing the personal question. Yet these challenges are interlinked. Religion is tainted by politics, politics is driven by private ambition, private happiness depends on spiritual satisfaction, and so on. The lack of specialization in the ancient world allows Lucretius to propose a coherent solution that addresses all facets of the challenge at the same time.

As an artifact, *The Nature of the Universe* seems alien to us today. We cannot imagine someone writing a seamless combination of science, philosophy, and poetry. At most, we can imagine a philosopher writing about science or a scientist writing about morality, but such a work would not exceed the bounds of specialized knowledge (the philosopher studies the philosophy of science, not science itself) or would present a mere curiosity (the scientist working as an amateur ethicist). We could never imagine someone writing a true combination of science and philosophy in *verse*. Why needlessly compound what is already a demanding task by writing dactylic hexameters? We tend to explain the oddity of ancient texts such as *The Nature of the Universe* in a patronizing way. "This is what science was like back then," we say to ourselves, or "This is how they wrote." We must keep reminding ourselves that *The Nature of the Universe* sprang naturally from the cultural life of the first century B.C. Readers of the time accepted the work on its own terms as an organic whole. They didn't think of it as pieced together from separate disciplines. That notion merely reflects our own preoccupation with specialization.

What would it take for us readers to imagine our world comprehensively just as Lucretius imagined his? We need the audacity to grapple with the big problems of our life and of the world, despite our own lack of expertise. We can allow ourselves to imagine, conjecture, fancy, and fabricate solutions—in other words, to use our freedom of thought and expression even if it takes us outside our comfort zone.

Suppose we take up the freedom to propose solutions to the world. Where would we get those ideas? Where would they come from? *Not from books, but from reading.* Books contain other people's ideas. We generate our own ideas through the friction of reading a text. The act of reading throws up ideas spontaneously much as wool rubbed over a glass rod creates a static charge. The eyes move smoothly across the page, but the soul resists the text, catches at it with a thousand microscopic fibers. What was that word? Does that idea make sense? Is this chapter relevant to me? Why did my mind wander to that particular daydream? Is this passage worth paying attention to? What would have been a better way to write it? What does it remind me of? What do I see in it? Does it give me pleasure? Do I prefer to dream my own dreams? The answers, in fragments, tumble pell-mell through our subconscious while the conscious mind heroically decodes the text. These ideas build up like an electric charge on the surface of our experience, waiting for us to assign them a direction, a pathway through which to discharge their tingling energy in a rush.

The imagination always tugs the reader in a different direction than the book and its author want to go. In a graduate class on the Beats, I once wrote a paper on the open-ended forms of postmodern poetry. I argued that traditional, closed forms of poetry (with uniform meters and rhyme schemes) restrict the imagination. Modern, open forms free the imagination to create new kinds of beauty and meaning. I took this line from William Blake as my keynote:

The cistern contains: the fountain overflows

My mind leapt to the conclusion that Blake scorned the stagnant water of the cistern (I may have confused the word with "cesspool") and celebrated the fountain's free-running water. My professor pointed out that a container of water possesses its own beauty, which is equal to, though different from, the beauty of the fountain. On reflection, I had to admit she was right. Blake's text does better support her interpretation than mine. With my hypothesis compromised, the energy drained out of my work. In conceding the point about the cistern, though, I had lost sight of a more important one. The wrong interpretation had inspired my research more than the right interpretation. I should have persisted in my mistake because it would have led to more discoveries about my subject than I made through acknowledgment of the most likely meaning of Blake's aphorism.

After the embarrassment of this incident, I noticed that my mind had a habit of leaping ahead of my sources whenever I would write papers. I would want to ground expansive claims on narrow support, perhaps a single, suggestive quotation or a quirky way of interpreting an author's words. At one point, I perceived depths of meaning in one line at the end of Joseph Conrad's *Heart of Darkness*. Marlowe has finished relating Kurtz's story of greed and brutality in Congo to Kurtz's fiancée. She says:

> You were with him—to the last? I think of his loneliness.
> Nobody near to understand him as I would have understood.
> Perhaps no one to hear ..."
>
> "To the very end," I said shakily. "I heard his very last words ..." I stopped in a fright.
>
> "Repeat them," she murmured in a heartbroken tone.
> "I want—I want—something—something—to—to live with."
>
> I was on the point of crying at her, "Don't you hear them?" The dusk was repeating them in a persistent whisper all around us, in a whisper that seemed to swell menacingly like the first whisper of a rising wind. "The horror! The horror!"
>
> "His last word—to live with," she insisted. "Don't you understand I loved him—I loved him—I loved him!"
>
> I pulled myself together and spoke slowly.
> "The last word he pronounced was—your name."

The last line entranced me. I analyzed it like verse. Conrad's prose flows so smoothly and surely. Even the dashes in preceding sentences add necessary pauses in the regular beat of Conrad's language. The flow underscores the vivid narration of the scene. We hear the words of all three speakers (Marlowe, the fiancée, and Kurtz) in direct discourse, not at second hand. Until, in the last two words, Marlowe stops and, instead of saying the fiancée's actual name, drops a paraphrase: "your name." Like a medium in a séance, he channels an alien voice. I imagine the words given leaden weight by accents on both syllables, Marlowe's voice falling in pitch and breaking off short with this spondee. He tosses the abstract category heading "names" into a recitation of specifics. It sits there out of place, contradicting the spirit of what had come before, cracking the storyteller's illusion. What is real in a story, it made me wonder?

This inconcinnity—the word I used back then—reveals a fissure in the smooth surface of the text where we can see the artifice of the narration. Not just the white lie to save the feelings of the fiancée but all of Marlowe's narrative and Conrad's, too. If we take the text at face value, it points to the dark reality of Africa's exploitation by colonial powers. Indeed, Belgium's extraction of resources from Congo during this time killed a million inhabitants. Conrad's direct, flowing narrative style presents this history to his readers as inevitable, whether we choose to confront the darkness frankly, read something redemptive into it, or simply prefer to look the other way. Yet the inconcinnity also indicates something else. When we read, the text itself becomes a kind of performance in our head, like the recitation of oral poetry by an ancient Greek rhapsode. The act of reading, of replaying the words in our mind, creates a reality of syllables and rhythm that stands in front of the reality of the story being narrated. The language is the immediate experience for us; the events it refers to are more distant. The text unfolds in its own distinct moment of reality, which stands just as far from the action in Congo as Homer's *Iliad* does from the Trojan War.

The artifice of the work frees us from the moral obligation that Conrad subtly imposes on us. A social crusader would have painted the horrors in Africa as starkly as possible in hopes of moving our conscience. Conrad knows we are expert at looking away from anything unpleasant. So he wraps the brutal events in a set of nesting narrative frames—the unnamed narrator of *Heart of Darkness* telling us about once hearing Marlowe relate the story on a yacht moored in the Thames, including an account of Marlowe's conversation with the fiancée. The framing conveniently places us at several removes from the horror in Congo so that we don't have to do it ourselves. At the same time, the framing makes explicit the filters we use to block out ugliness. Conrad taunts us: "I'm making it easy for you to ignore the horror, but you know it's still there anyway. Do you have the moral courage to penetrate these filters and confront reality directly?"

As a reader, I do not have to answer Conrad's challenge any more than he had to pose it. I allow myself the same freedom of choice that he enjoyed as an author. I do not have to take *Heart of Darkness* on his terms. I have my own concerns. I will extract from the work whatever I can in order to solve the problems that I face today. Back then, I needed help developing my own writing style. I gave myself permission to study the rhythm of

Conrad's prose rather than to piously interpret "the horror." I wanted to emulate the polish of his sentences (I still do). Yet another, rawer voice punches through this smooth surface in the phrase "your name." It hints at a darker personality lurking in the depths that maybe Conrad couldn't control or wasn't even aware of. I learned to listen for multiple voices in a text whereas before I acknowledged only the author's voice and assumed he commanded every nuance. I began to hear new depths in language. It became a drama rather than a communication stream.

I could never write a formal essay on the subject of "your name" because I loaded too much meaning onto two little words. I infused them with my own subjective thoughts. To turn my insight into scholarship, I would have had to do considerable background reading, including what Conrad said about *Heart of Darkness* and this passage (if anything), how critics have interpreted it, and what scholars have said about Conrad's prose style. Perhaps, I would have found no support for my point of view, and even if I did, the journals to which I would submit my article could easily reject it as trivial. The amount of work required and the uncertainty of the results meant that I never bothered to develop the idea further. Doing so seemed beside the point, anyway. The insight intrigued me. I played with it in my head for years. I looked at other passages in other writers from this perspective. In other words, the idea served my purposes. It solved a personal problem. That was its palpable value. I didn't need anyone else to validate it.

Mistaken ideas are just as vivid as accurate ideas, probably more vivid, because they express the deep wishes of our heart—our desires, hopes, fears, and pathologies. Misreadings furnish the vocabulary of our soul. They describe our soul's needs. Through them, the energy of the unconscious erupts into our waking life. Misreading makes visible the ideas thrown up by our soul's faculty of resistance to the text. This faculty works through indirection. We set out to study one thing, say, Conrad's *Heart of Darkness*, and it subtly shifts our attention to something else, the polyphony of language. The intellect goes straight at its object and demands accurate ideas about it. I cannot learn anything demonstrable about *Heart of Darkness* unless I gather facts and apply logic. By contrast, the imagination introduces a third term. It uses *Heart of Darkness* as a means to get at its own topic of interest. For this maneuver, accuracy doesn't matter. Insight matters, the glimpse of a new vista, a mad idea which we try to shake away yet which keeps tickling us until we pay attention.

The value we derive from reading depends hardly at all on the quality of the text; rather, it depends on the quality of our reading and what we do afterward. The only measure of success is whether reading makes a difference in our lives. If we "click" with the text and become receptive to the ideas our mind spontaneously generates in reading it, we can create great value for ourselves and those around us. If the text doesn't speak to us and we experience nothing remarkable, it holds no value for us, no matter how great a masterpiece it is. Let the book prove its worth through what it does for us. I once knew a woman who grew up in Nicolai Ceauşescu's repressive Romania and who fervently declared of Paolo Coelho's *The Alchemist*, "That book changed my life!" Kirkus Reviews describes it as "an interdenominational, transcendental, inspirational fable—in other words, a bag of wind … The absence of characterization and overall blandness suggest authorship by a committee of self-improvement pundits …."[1] The woman went off to central Asia to work on women's issues for the United Nations. Bad literature spurred her to valuable service; it did not detract from the richness of her life. Only a fool would tell her, "You should have read Henry David Thoreau's *Walden*, instead!"

The notion that value resides in the book imprisons us. We start to read great literature because we believe it will do us good, and we often become captive to the first compelling ideas we find in it. We grab onto those ideas for dear life and never let them go. We ask no further questions. We don't see a point in trying to find a way around the cultural authority we have erected to rule over us. I taught for a year at a university in the Bible Belt. I once posed this question to a class:

> The U.S. Constitution guarantees you freedom of religion, and you can choose from maybe hundreds of religions: Judaism, Islam, Hinduism, Buddhism, and so on. There are dozens and dozens of Christian sects alone. How many of you have chosen a different religion from the one your parents have?

No one raised a hand. I suppose that if I had asked about politics, I would have gotten a similar response. So often, on the most important questions of our lives, we simply accept the positions that we inherited from our parents or cultural traditions. We have a vast number of options. We have the freedom to choose. But we don't exercise it. We prefer a specious certainty over the risk of exercising our creativity.

We misapply most of the apparatus of reading, including critical theories, toward helping us locate meaning in the text rather than in ourselves. We must employ a different class of tools to do the latter. These tools serve to amplify the ideas sparked by the friction of the text moving through our mind so that we can better evaluate them and put them to use. To start with, we must find some rapport with the books that we read just as my acquaintance did with *The Alchemist*. I almost never read a book unless it appeals to my soul in some way. I seldom give in to idle curiosity, homework assignments, people's recommendations, and other rationalistic means of deciding what to read. Instead, I approach books as I would other works of art—I allow pleasure, instinct, and intuition to draw me to them just I do with the paintings I view and the music I listen to. The books I choose project some image, however small, that I feel compelled to explore. I do not pick books for utilitarian reasons, but they always end up bearing on some problem I happen to be wrestling with at the time. No one assigned *Heart of Darkness* to me. I read it because it satisfied my appetite.

In this way, books become symbols for meanings or discoveries we need to articulate about ourselves and our world. "A symbol," according to psychologist C.G. Jung, "always presupposes that the chosen expression is the best possible description or formulation of a relatively unknown fact, which is none the less known to exist or is postulated as existing."[2] Reading occurs on the interface between the world we know and the world that remains as yet unknown. Every discovery made about the latter modifies our perceptions of the former. We conjecture new relationships between the things that make up our world. As a result, familiar terms lose their accuracy, and we must invent a vocabulary to describe the new phenomenon. We generate that vocabulary through the experience of reading. A misinterpreted aphorism or two words that stick out oddly at the end of a story give us something tangible to manipulate with our mind until it yields the insight we need.

We cultivate such symbols by adopting reading techniques that throw us off balance. New ideas do not arise in the center of our attention but on the periphery. When we read, the storyline or the argument holds our attention, so we must make a deliberate effort to shift our eyes to the outer rim of consciousness. A traditional method for doing so involves treating the text as an oracle. A suppliant comes to an oracle looking for the solution to a problem. The oracle responds with a gnomic, almost nonsensical answer. The suppliant then finds some way to apply this answer to his problem. An oracle works by introducing an element of chance into our thoughts, thereby allowing space for solutions to emerge from unexpected quarters. An oracle could take many forms, including that of a randomly selected passage in the Bible or some other book. Another technique involves looking at the text in detail. Language possesses a metaphorical quality in its most granular elements. Every word exhibits a unique range of meaning as well as relationships with other words and concepts. Writers usually compose a text to narrow each word to one unambiguous sense. Readers do not have to accept the writer's intention. They can mentally substitute words as I did with "cistern" and "cesspool," or they can inject into the text the other nuances and connections that a given word may exhibit in other contexts. These word games empower the reader's imagination to change directions and go somewhere he prefers rather than continuing to follow the writer's line of argument.

Above all, we can test the meaning of a book with our own lives. Alexander the Great imagined that he was the reincarnation of Achilles from Homer's *Iliad*. During battle, Alexander would jump into the fray to fight with the enemy hand to hand—an insane risk for a general to take. His death could cause the army to disintegrate. But the impulse makes sense if you are trying to reprise the role of Achilles and you imagine you have his invulnerability and destiny. The political career of Paul Ryan, Speaker of the U.S. House of Representatives, looks like an attempt to enact the ideas of Ayn Rand's *Atlas Shrugged*, which shaped his world view from the time he was in college. In Rand's novel, businessmen go on strike to protest the burdens placed on them by the government. In Rand's view, only entrepreneurs create wealth for society through their imagination and drive. The envious and less gifted use the government to take what businessmen have made. As Speaker, Ryan pushed through large tax cuts for the wealthy and corporations. By freeing them from some of their government-imposed burdens, he expected them to be able to create more wealth for society.

Ordinary readers can test books in the world, too. I know people who took a canoe trip in Massachusetts and New Hampshire to retrace the journey that Thoreau describes in *A Week on the Concord and Merrimack Rivers*. Thousands of people have read the book, but only a few have made that trip. It's easy to read a book. It costs far more in time, money, and risk to reenact it as my friends did. We expend the energy to overcome our inertia when we believe the value of the book lies in something beyond its message or interpretation. In reading it, we see a possibility for our own lives, which we hadn't seen before. We feel the urge to test it. We want to experiment with ourselves. We slip the book in our pocket and go out the door.

Serious readers feel an urge toward reality, a need to validate the ideas that we base our life on. We long to test what we have read against the physical and social reality of the world at large. We want to see whether the places and people we read about are as we imagined them to be. That is why we take the risk of experiments which can fail or turn out quite differently from what we expect. Inevitably, the world falsifies some of our ideas. Ideas we held sacred fall apart under examination so that we must search for new ones. Cultural institutions decay beyond repair, and new ones must be built. Marx and Engels say it best:

> All fixed, fast-frozen relations, with their train of ancient and venerable prejudices and opinions are swept away, all new-formed ones become antiquated before they can ossify. All that is solid melts into air, all that is holy is profaned, and man is at last compelled to face with sober senses his real conditions of life, and his relations with his kind.[3]

In the end, we discover that we do not live in a world of refractory physical and social structures; rather, we inhabit the malleable meanings attached to them. The world always remains open, never defined once and for all. Therefore, we do not have to suffer the world merely; we can reimagine it into many forms. The images we conjure from a text furnish the primordial substance of the human universe, which we can refashion as we choose.

NOTES

1 Kirkus Reviews, 1 May 1993, www.kirkusreviews.com/book-reviews/paulo-coelho/the-alchemist/.
2 C.G. Jung, *Psychological Types*, tr. R.F.C. Hull and H.G. Baynes (Princeton, NJ: Princeton University Press, 1971), p. 474.
3 Karl Marx and Friedrich Engels, *The Communist Manifesto*, tr. Samuel Moore (New York: Penguin Books, 1967), p. 83.

PART I

The experience of reading

CHAPTER 2

Reading as a dream

I pissed off one of the few notable writers I have ever met. The poet Gwendolyn Brooks came to give a reading at a nearby university when I was in graduate school. Eastern Connecticut State University lies just outside of Willimantic, Connecticut. I can remember driving down Route 32 on a sunny evening in April. The winding road and tree-covered hills of rural Connecticut, punctuated by rocky outcrop-pings, gave way to the green lawns and streets of a more suburban neighborhood. The reading took place in a brightly lit auditorium that was only a little bigger and better furnished than one you can find in a middle-class high school. Gwendolyn Brooks attracted a good crowd, including high school students and college students as well as grad students like me. At that time, she was one of the few contemporary poets I liked apart from the Beat and Black Mountain poets. I chose an aisle seat near the front, and Brooks read from a podium on the stage:

> They eat beans mostly, this old yellow pair,
> Dinner is a casual affair.
> Plain chipware on a plain and creaking wood,
> Tin flatware.
>
> Two who are Mostly Good.
> Two who have lived their day,
> But keep on putting on their clothes
> And putting things away.
>
> And remembering ...
> Remembering, with twinklings and twinges,
> As they lean over the beans in their rented back room that is full of
>   beads and receipts and dolls and cloths, tobacco crumbs, vases
>   and fringes.[1]

Like any well-known poet, Brooks knew how to perform. She would voice the unstressed syllables slowly but with gathering momentum, then quickly speak the stressed syllable with sharply rising pitch, in exaggerated singsong rhythms:

They eat **beans mostly**, this old **yellow pair** ...

When she finished reading, she stepped down into the orchestra pit to talk to anyone who wanted to come forward to say hello. A semicircle soon formed around her. I could see her benevolence. I waited my turn, then nervously asked, "Where do the voices in your poems come from?"

"I hear them in my head," she said. "They come from the people around me."

"But people don't really talk like that, in a sing-song voice," I pressed.

She glared at me. She suspected an insult and doubtless wondered what this young, white kid in rural Connecticut could possibly know about the people she had experienced as a black woman from Chicago over 40 years his senior. "I hope not sing-song!" she said, still glaring. I turned away so as not to annoy her further.

I had discovered—and my encounter with Gwendolyn Brooks confirmed—that the voice we hear in our head when we're reading differs from the voice of people speaking aloud. For comparison, we can more easily imagine a level conversational tone if we look at the poem reduced to prose form:

> They eat beans mostly, this old yellow pair. Dinner is a casual affair, plain chipware on a plain and creaking wood, tin flatware. Two who are mostly good, two who have lived their day, but keep on putting on their clothes and putting things away. And remembering ... remembering, with twinklings and twinges as they lean over the beans in their rented back room that is full of beads and receipts and dolls and cloths, tobacco crumbs, vases and fringes.

Imagine a newscaster delivering this script. He speaks in sentences or phrases rather than lines of verse. He utters them with a frank intonation that emphasizes the meaning of the syntactical units. He wants to convey that meaning to you as plainly as possible and does not want to distract you by modulating the sound of his voice. So, he speaks matter-of-factly, hitting a single syllable in every phrase to give the lines a flatter contour:

They eat **beans** mostly, this **old** yellow pair.

The newscaster views the text as a connected whole. All of the sentences and phrases within it join into a coherent argument. The viewers don't understand fully until he has delivered the entire passage, so he keeps driving forward in his reading. He pauses briefly only when he needs a breath. He doesn't have time to gather its force for unusual emphasis at any point. He ignores the playful combinations of sounds. His voice goes right over "twinklings and twinges" without apparent consciousness of the initial rhyme. He maintains a reporter's factual tone when he lists "beads and receipts and dolls and cloths, tobacco crumbs, vases and fringes." He makes no judgment— no leap of the imagination—about what these items add up to. He provides only an objective report and leaves listeners to interpret it for themselves.

But Brooks formatted the text as a poem. The short lines and extra punctuation interrupt us if we try to read it straight off like prose. "They eat beans mostly," [pause] "this old yellow pair," [longer pause] "Dinner is a casual affair." [stop] Verse invites us to slow down and pay attention. We have time to absorb all the possibilities. They don't just happen to be eating beans; they eat beans because they are poor. They are not two individuals with an indeterminate relationship; they are a "pair," bonded closely together. They are "yellow," sallow, overdone by age. The sound of the verse further colors the meaning. The longer first line ending in "pair" rhymes with the shorter second line ending in "affair." The rhyme hits us too soon, brings the second line to an abrupt stop soon after it gets going to reflect a meal shortened because there is not much to eat. The rhyme is also a bit pat as though the pair had shared such a meal for so many years it offers nothing new to savor. We hear the irony of "casual affair," which underlines the lack of choice this couple has, with their chipped plates and shabby rented room. A formal dinner party is out of the question. They do linger over their memories, emphasized by the repeated four-syllable word and the ellipsis: "And remembering …/Remembering." In this soundscape, "twinklings and twinges" takes on greater poignancy. The couple's eyes sparkle when they recall happy times, and they feel pangs of regret for what they have lost or wished they had done differently. The two words rhyme as these aspects of a shared past go inevitably together. They are also cutesy words, hinting at the fond, private language of this pair. And the final line—more than twice as long as any other in the poem—lays out their souvenirs of life, the tangible fragments left over from decades together, each item capable of sustaining its own poem, perhaps a whole book, if only we knew its story.

I have translated the sounds of this poem into rational ideas in order to demonstrate the potential of Brooks' verse. In doing so, I risk reducing "The Bean Eaters" to a coded message, whose true meaning lies in my interpretation rather than in the words themselves. We also risk becoming paralyzed with fascination at the artistry of a poet like Brooks who can make such a small number of words paint a fully realized scene. In fact, the meaning of a poem comes from its sound or at least the way the sounds interact with the denotation of its words. Those sounds create feelings in us readers. We do not merely understand the poem; we experience it. Doubtless, we each feel the poem a bit differently because we fit it into our own unique lives. Some of us experience the poem more richly than others, depending on the imagination we apply. However that may be, the reader's feeling *is* the meaning. We feel the meaning. We lose sight of the value of the poem if we insist that Brooks meant this or the text means that to all readers. We must put aside the analytical language of criticism, which we learn in school, and develop instead a subjective language for teasing our experience of a text into full view.

Let's return to the way Brooks heard this poem, which I characterized as singsong. We could not deduce it from the bare text. Certainly, the poem consists of stressed and unstressed syllables arranged to form a rhythm, and readers can replicate that rhythm accurately in their head when they read. Brooks the poet knew the craft of verse-making and created this rhythm deliberately. Nevertheless, Brooks also read her own text—we think of authors strictly as the writers of a text, ignoring the fact that they also read it. Brooks the reader, without knowing it, heard other sounds in her verse beside the ones she had explicitly fashioned. The peculiar nature of her mind distorted the rhythmic conventions of poetry. At her appearance in Willimantic, she meant to deliver "The Bean Eaters" the way she had constructed it, but her performance unwittingly divulged the odd voice in her head.

We all distort the sounds of words in our head, especially when we read silently. In silent reading, time speeds up. The text becomes detached from clock time and instead rushes along like the syncopated images in a dream. The mind can move faster than the tongue, vocal chords, and breath in articulating the words. Most people can read 250–300 words a minute silently at a comfortable pace, but we can speak or read aloud comfortably at only about 120–150 words a minute. Silent reading also exaggerates, almost idealizes the mannerisms of speech. The orator's intonations become more colorful, more deeply felt. The emphatic parts attain a ringing power, the quiet parts a delicate purity. The lover pleads more ardently. The criminal excuses himself with sweeter reason. The sentences we voice in our heads follow speech contours we could never use aloud without sounding stilted, pompous, unnatural. The usual pattern of stresses shifts around to accentuate different syllables, and odd rhythms form.

Yet all of this strange soundscape seems perfectly natural when we have immersed ourselves in silent reading. Our internal reading voice differs from a speaking voice much as the action of our dreams differs from the action of people in the physical world. In our dreams, the harder we run, the slower we move. We fly. We talk but no one hears us. We switch locations instantly. Emotion suffuses the dreamscape; our experience is bathed in love, beauty, anger, and terror. All of these actions seem normal or at least inevitable while we're dreaming. Only after we wake and return to the expectations of the physical world does the dream action, already fading from consciousness, seem distorted and funny. Similarly, when we are reading silently, the voices of the text running through our head sound perfectly normal and inevitable. From habit, as soon as we pick up a book, we instantly drop into a full, self-consistent world which encloses our attention so thoroughly that the world of physical sound never touches it. The contrast between the sound of language in our head and the sound of spoken language never emerges into our consciousness. Either we concentrate on our book and block out ambient noise, or the noise and voices around us distract us from our reading. Without any obvious juxtaposition, we don't realize silent reading has different rules and behaviors from the physical world. Only those who listen closely, like poets, hear the strange rhythms of a text unfolding in their head. Even then they may not realize how differently the internal and external voices sound.

Reading involves a rapport with the text that we seldom acknowledge. We typically think of the text as giving us something—a meaning. But we supply the text with something as well—animation. The poet Robert Creeley describes teaching poetry to a student "who in truth could perceive no demonstrable difference between a cluster of words called *poem* and a cluster of words called *prose*."

> She felt the typographical form of the poem was all that apparently defined it—and that of course was a very arbitrary gimmick, to her mind. I tried everything, "Mary had a little lamb," tum te tum, clapped my hands with the beat, pulled out the vowels à la Yeats, probably even sang. Still it stayed flat and arbitrary. She felt the beat and texture of the sound was imposed by the will of the reader and was not initial in the words themselves. All the usual critical terms were of course useless, far too abstract. Finally I truly despaired of gaining more than her sympathy and patience. Then one day, we were

> reading Edward Marshall's "Leave the Word Alone," and for
> some immaculate and utterly unanticipated "reason" she *got*
> it, she heard all the play of rhythms and sounds bringing that
> extraordinary statement of primary humanness into such a
> density of feeling and song.[2]

I have no idea whether "the play of rhythms and sounds" that she heard in the poem was the same as the one Creeley heard or the one Marshall had engineered. That is like asking whether the yellow paint on a wall looks the same to you as it does to me. The point is, she developed a deeper connection with the text than her rational mind admitted. Something had switched on inside her. She felt possibilities that hadn't existed previously for her. She intuited an organic pattern in the language which the printed words alone did not denote. This intuition transformed the text from a mere message into a deeply moving experience, comparable to what Creeley and Marshall felt.

When we read to ourselves, we reach down into our minds to the level of spontaneous creativity with language. There language possesses numinous energy. We hear the voices of gods as we reenact in our head the text on the page. Divine personas project through the words as they play out in our mind. These personas seem larger, more sharply cut than the literal meaning of the sentences would indicate. Each narrative voice, each character sounds as the archetype of itself. We don't consciously inflate its language with god-like qualities; it emerges spontaneously from deeper in our soul. This divine energy fascinates us and compels our attention.

Prose with a strong personality induces a trance in the reader. Sentence after sentence rolls by. We gradually relax the disbelief with which we approach a text. The rhythm of the words lulls our critical faculties to sleep until we have delivered ourselves over to the ups and downs of the language. Reading thereby changes the very rhythm of our own thoughts. If we put down the book and pick up a pen, we find that we are writing in the author's style rather than our own. I have had such dreamlike experiences from reading Ralph Waldo Emerson:

> Our age is retrospective. It builds the sepulchres of the fathers.
> It writes biographies, histories, and criticism. The foregoing
> generations beheld God and nature face to face; we, through
> their eyes. Why should not we also enjoy an original relation to
> the universe? Why should not we have a poetry and philosophy
> of insight and not of tradition, and a religion by revelation to us,
> and not a history of theirs? Embosomed for a season in nature,

whose floods of life stream around and through us, and invite
us by the powers they supply, to action proportioned to nature,
why should we grope among the dry bones of the past, or put
the living generation into masquerade out of its faded ward-
robe? The sun shines to-day also. There is more wool and flax
in the fields. There are new lands, new men, new thoughts. Let
us demand our own works and laws and worship.[3]

Reading alters our consciousness because it fuses the conceptual and
the physical. The rhythm of a well-written piece makes us feel that we
can move in time to it. This sense of rhythm permits us to enter into
the frame of mind out of which the writer's thoughts sprang. The idea
a writer wants to convey becomes as persuasive as any experience. For
this reason, Emerson does not expound his thought in straightforward,
clinical prose. If he had, he could have expressed himself more suc-
cinctly since there's really only one idea here: "Don't let tradition keep
you from original discoveries about the world." Any such attempt to
paraphrase his text sounds flat; it misses the essential ingredient.

Emerson's language gives us a chance to practice his philosophy.
Emerson maintained that we don't have to go anywhere or flee from the
world to find significance; the here and now will do. The objects of life
point toward meanings that transcend the mundane. We need to reflect on
these signs, to keep circling back over them in our minds, until they yield
the insight we need. The rhythm of Emerson's prose reenacts this process
as he circles back over his idea sentence by sentence, clause by clause. The
passage starts with simple declarative sentences of gradually increasing
length, the first with one adjective in the predicate ("retrospective"), the
second with two nouns ("sepulchers," "fathers"), and the third with three
("biographies," "histories," "criticism"). Then follows a series of "why"
questions whose length increases through a similar addition of elements
in each succeeding sentence. Finally, the passage recurs to simple declarative sentences, the first with one element in the predicate, the second
with two elements, and the third with three elements ("new lands, new
men, new thoughts"). And Emerson caps the passage with an exhortation
whose three predicate elements ("our own works and law and worship")
repeat the rhythm of the penultimate sentence. The one-two-three repeating rhythm draws the reader without realizing it into Emerson's way
of viewing the world. Emerson starts with assertions so obvious, or at
any rate so simple, that we don't dispute them. Then, the gradual building of elements and complexity invisibly crosses the boundary from fact
to meaning, from description to urging—join me in demanding new
structures to match our new lives in this new world. The three-element

rhyme of the last two sentences makes Emerson's polite command seem perfectly reasonable, even unavoidable.

The effect of Emerson's rhetoric builds lick by lick so that by the end of the paragraph, we have participated in the subtlety and depth of Emerson's philosophy. Read a few pages of Emerson with some attention, and his incantatory phrasing convinces you utterly because you have not simply listened to his ideas, you have entered into the experience of thinking them.

On one or two occasions, I have drifted into sleep while reading Emerson, induced by the hypnotic succession of his sentences. Not the sleep of boredom, but the sleep in which inner eyes open when outer eyes close. I still held the book in my hands and directed my gaze at it. I did not realize my eyelids had shut, so I continued "reading" Emerson in my head. In my sleep, I seemed to follow with my eyes the black lines of his text on the white page. My mind, as active as if I were awake, picked up and carried forward the stream of Emerson's thoughts, adding inference after inference, example after example, analogy after analogy. And I expressed those ideas in Emersonian sentences, which just flowed in my mind like prophecy. I seemed to "read" Emerson and create original thoughts indistinguishably. I felt as though I had caught the secret of oratory from Emerson's words and could prophesy in the same vein. I know people who have had the same experience with this author.

Consciousness follows a kind of rhythm, and when we read with any attention, this mental rhythm aligns itself to the rhythm of the text. A text looks like a series of discrete words. We often think about reading as decoding first one element and then another and another until we understand the message. But the reader's mind doesn't experience a text that way. We read a text just as we experience anything that unfolds over time. William James describes it this way:

> The unit of composition of our perception of time is a *duration*, with a bow and a stern, as it were—a rearward- and a forward-looking end. It is only as parts of this *duration-block* that the relation of *succession* of one end to the other is perceived. We do not first feel one end and then feel the other after it, and from the perception of the succession infer an interval of time between, but we seem to feel the interval of time as a whole, with the two ends embedded in it.[4]

In other words, our perception of the world does not unfold in a series of discrete elements; rather, the sense of flow inheres in each element of consciousness. Think of Emerson's sentences as duration blocks.

Their brevity occupies a single moment of our attention. Their simple syntax and parallelism contain a beginning and an end. We feel the heave at the start of a sentence, and we feel the point rounded off at its end. Thus, each sentence is an integral whole whose rhythm measures out a unit of time. Not the identical units ticked off mechanically by a clock but units whose variable lengths and relationships with each other we feel intuitively. We mark time with our minds. We measure the duration of the sentence we are reading at this moment in comparison to the length of the preceding sentences. And so we move along, with each new sentence occupying the center of our attention while sentences we have recently read gradually fade from our memory. The contour that these durations form stays in our consciousness longer than the sentences' meaning:

> A simple sensation, as we shall hereafter see, is an abstraction, and all our concrete states of mind are representations of objects with some amount of complexity. Part of the complexity is the echo of the objects just past, and, in a less degree, perhaps the foretaste of those just to arrive. Objects fade out of consciousness slowly. If the present thought is of ABCDEFG, the next one with be of BCDEFGH, and the one after that of CDEFGHI—the lingerings of the past dropping successively away, and the incomings of the future making up the loss. These lingerings of old objects, these incomings of new, are the germs of memory and expectation, the retrospective and prospective sense of time. They give that continuity to consciousness without which it could not be called a stream.[5]

The rhythms of a text like Emerson's mimic the stream of consciousness that any of us experience. Our own stream of consciousness adapts to its environment. It turns the myriad stimuli that our senses receive into a regular tempo that our mind can make sense of. This is how we negotiate with the world at large. The stream of consciousness moves slowly when we are relaxed or tired, fast when something exciting goes on around us and the adrenaline pumps. It adjusts to the cadence of what we read, too, especially if the passage exhibits moderate regularity as Emerson's does. A perfectly regular text repeating, say, a one- or two-element sentence pattern would be monotonous and cause us to slumber. A text with sentence patterns that vary too widely would keep us awake but won't enchant us. Emerson's 1–2–3, 1–2–3 pattern hypnotizes us. Our mind stays awake even as we drift into sleep.

Language flows dreamlike into and out of all of us. Language rolls through our minds like a mighty subterranean river that rises to the surface of our consciousness here and there on occasion. The Emersonian rhetorical phrases that I heard or composed in my sleep arose in some primal level of awareness where creation, imitation, and consumption have not become distinct. From this perspective, the division between reader and writer seems arbitrary. I described my experience of *reading* Emerson in my sleep. If I had written down the phantom Emersonian lines I had composed in my head, I could have called myself a writer. At their origin in the bottom of our minds, reading and writing spring from the same spontaneous process rather than constitute the distinct functions they appear to in the waking world. The linguistic potential of authors and readers is the same.

Indeed, my subconscious has come up with more original work. Here's a snatch of language that I dreamed one morning when I had emerged from deep slumber but had not fully awoken. I surfed in delicious half-sleep for as long as I wished. During this time, I kept repeating these words in my head because I liked the way they sounded:

> All things are beautiful ... in its own time. Even the word of the poet
>   are sufficient for a lover.

The words don't make sense for readers trained in correct English. The meaning is not obvious, and both sentences miss on subject/verb agreement. Nevertheless, the passage is suggestive. First, it had a definite tonal contour. The first part sounded sententious, elevated, followed by a pause for emphasis and then a shorter passage with the stress on "own." The second sentence had a rising cadence that peaked at the word "poet," followed by a descending cadence that resolved the sentiment. As I headed toward consciousness, the sentences crystallized into a stanza:

> All things are beautiful
>   ... in its *own* time;
>   even the word of the poet
> Are sufficient for a lover.

You can believe that the lines belong in a stanza because they have just about the same size if you count the pause at the start of line 2 as a beat. The passage has a shape, a plural–singular/singular–plural symmetry. The shape alludes to a common conceit about the nature of the cosmos—is it one or many? The second line implies that the things which make up the cosmos move or develop according to an inherent rhythm. The heightened rhetoric carries over into the second half with "the word." The singular suggests a cosmic significance ("In the beginning was the word …") or some other grand meaning ("a man's word is his bond"). The passage also ties these big themes to human experience. The word "even" points to a connection between the cosmos in the first two lines and the world of poetry in lines 3 and 4. The implied rhythms of the poet echo the rhythm of the cosmos. We can glimpse the cosmic "word" in the actual words (the implied subject of "are sufficient") of a poet. These words reassure the "lover," a universal role we have all played at some time. Finally, the passage is reflexive. We ourselves experience the words and rhythms that these four lines talk about, including both their human and their cosmic meanings, by virtue of reading them.

In this episode, was I a reader or a writer? On one hand, I wrote the words down and present them to you now on the page. As far as you know, I am their author. On the other hand, the passage came to me from I don't know where, although it contains hints about possible antecedents such as the Gospel of John. I didn't consciously compose it the way I compose this sentence right now. I absorbed it passively just as readers passively absorb the text that they find on the page. The passage played over and over in my head much as when we come across a striking line in a book and repeat it to ourselves, mulling its significance. In my head, the words originally formed a mere rhythmic line or sequence that I heard, but I then wanted to visualize the way they would appear if they were printed and I were the reader. The four-line stanza seemed the natural, inevitable form the passage should take, not a deliberate artistic choice of my own. I performed the role of writer simply by anticipatory reading. If I had never written the words down, which could easily have been the case, I would never have thought of myself as the passage's "author."

Writers don't deserve the reverence we give to their creativity. The subconscious flow of language feeds writers no more than it does readers. They enjoy no special access to language that readers lack. Where did Emerson get his language? Like Gwendolyn Brooks or me or anyone else, he heard the speech of ordinary people. He listened to other Unitarian preachers of his day. He read Emanuel Swedenborg. And so on and so forth. Creativity with language starts from absorbing the rhythms of the sentences we hear or read, transmuting them in the uniqueness of our minds (often without us realizing it), and uttering words in a new form. Those words in turn become the raw material for others' creativity.

I liken this process to chain mail. Chain mail consists of a network of small metal loops. Each loop links with, say, six other loops, so that, link by link, row by row, the chain mail grows into a continuous fabric in the shape of a vest, pants, or some other garment that a soldier can wear for protection. Each loop supports and is supported by the loops it is attached to. Similarly, each reader or writer linguistically influences, and receives influences from, many other people, and each of them, in turn, exerts influences on several further individuals, and so on until a continuous fabric of language weaves across society and over time. Ultimately, only a few writers occupy positions in this mesh of language. Readers contribute many more links, and those who seldom write or read account for still more of the chain mail. Authors are not fundamentally more important in this fabric than readers or nonreaders. We all influence and are influenced by others. We all alternate between "odd" and "normal" forms of language such as I described above with Brooks and Emerson. We all dream, and we all wake. The particular medium of these influences, whether print or speech, counts less than the network of influences as a whole. We violate the integrity of the fabric of language when we pick out one category of practitioner, the authors, and value their influence more than the other links. Writing is not a more important function than reading, speaking, and listening.

I want the chain mail metaphor to replace our classic understanding of inspiration. Plato likened inspiration to the magnetism that travels in one direction from a lodestone through a series of metal links attached to it. The force comes from the originating lodestone or authorial genius and is passively received by the links or readers. We usually explain literary tradition in this unidirectional fashion. We start with a great author, say, John Milton, and we trace his influence on a series of lesser writers over time. When we study literature, we focus on the most influential writers, that is, the writers from whom we can trace the longest chains. When we do so, though, we are just being selective in our attention. We isolate one loop or row in what is, in fact, a fabric of mail and accord it undue importance. Some of the loops may shine more brightly than others; nevertheless, they function only when connected all together in a mesh. That mesh is a collective unconscious to which we all, readers and writers alike, stake an equal claim. The dreams that blossom from it for readers matter as much as the dreams of authors.

This equivalence contrasts with the subordinate relationship that reader has traditionally had to writer. It seems almost too obvious to state that writers are cultural authorities. I went to see Gwendolyn Brooks;

she didn't come to see me. I expected to learn from her. I respected the fact that she had published many books of poetry. She had won a reputation among critics of contemporary verse. I knew it would be "good for me" to go. In short, I fell naturally into the subordinate role of the reader or student. I did not reflect that this transaction required me to set aside my own linguistic dreams in order to admire hers.

We experience a text as vividly as we do dreams, where images tantalize the senses. Readers encounter words first as physical objects. They convey sensory impressions. Like any tangible object, they possess a specific shape and size, based on the font, ink, and vagaries of printing. They have color—even black comes in a range of shades if you look closely. The quality of the paper they appear on gives them texture. Every book exhibits its own particular contrast between the ink—how dark? how thick? sharp characters or curvy ones?—and the paper—white or beige? matte or glossy? coarse-grained or fine? Paper and ink also produce a scent. I like to stick my nose in the middle of an open book, close my eyes, and slowly inhale to savor the smell. I suppose you can even put the words in your mouth to taste if you want. These characteristics carry an emotional tone inextricable from the empirical sensations. The physical properties of words help set the mood in which we read and, therefore, color our experience of the text, the way we perceive it, and ultimately the meaning we derive from it.

These physical properties shimmer before our sight like dream images. Words engage our senses, but they do not allow us to reach out and enfold them with our arms. They elude us when we try to address them in the direct, tactile way in which we deal with the waking world. Dreams move us more by the sequencing of images and by the emotions that accompany them. In reading, that level of experience emerges from the phonology of words, blending the physical with meaning. Words consist of syllables or articulate sounds. Some individual syllables coincide with distinct ideas, such as "I," "run," and "here." Most exhibit greater potential for meaning if they combine (kəm BĪN′) to form words.

When we read, strings of syllables fuse into an organic whole with a tempo and a sound contour. Say these words to yourself, pausing for a couple of seconds between each one to give it its individual weight: "our"—"age"—"is"—"retrospective." The first three one-syllable words carry a primary stress while the fourth word has a primary stress on the first syllable and a secondary stress on the third. Now, put them together in a sentence: "Our age is retrospective." The stresses have changed. "Age" still carries a primary stress; but "our" now has a secondary stress, and "is" has lost its stress. The first and third syllables of "retrospective" have swapped their stresses—the third syllable carries the primary stress, with the first syllable becoming secondary. The shift in stresses turns these four individual words into one integral phrase (a "duration block" as James put it). Instead of the monotone of speaking one discrete word after another, the four words recognize each other, so to speak, and modify their voices to become a unit. "Our" reduces its stress to emphasize the stress on its noun "age." "Is" drops its stress altogether to join the two elements on either side. The primary stress shifts to the penultimate syllable of "retrospective" in acknowledgment that it rounds off a sentence and needs to place the emphasis nearer its end. In ordinary speech, the modified stress contour indicates that these words go together and should be interpreted this way.

The colloquial way of pronouncing a phrase isn't the only possible way, however. Composing phrases creates intonations that form a rhythm, and rhythm expresses emotion. These rhythms draw us along and enfold us in a sonic world implying many possible meanings. Instead of this standard pronunciation:

Our **age** is retro**spec**tive.

We could also try putting the stress on the first word:

Our age is retro**spec**tive.

Or the third word:

Our age **is** retro**spec**tive.

Or we could try turning it into anapests:

Our age **is** retro**spec**tive.

Or:

Our age **is** retrospec**tive**.

We can play with the intonations of this sentence endlessly as we might in a dream, circling back and back in search of some significance that lies hidden there we can't quite grasp. Each of these intonations suggests some different shade of meaning. Do we emphasize *our* generation, distinct from other generations? Do we assert that it *is* retrospective against people who call it forward-looking? Do we try some quirky pronunciation to mock the idea or to shake loose some unexpected insight from it? With the last version, we realize that "is" and "-tive" rhyme. Throwing this attention on the least remarkable syllables highlights their grammatical function. Is our entire age epitomized in this one, present moment of "is?" Is "retrospective" not just a quality of our age but the defining characteristic? Or is "retrospective" a noun? We wander into all sorts of plausible and implausible suppositions, which contain the seeds of ideas.

The potential we sense in this not-just-sound/not-fully-meaning phenomenon of rhythm invites our creativity. What do we hear in the text? It could come from our own unconscious, or it could echo something we heard someone else say in another context entirely. We do not have to aim at what the author meant or hunt for a predetermined meaning. Freed from the burden of having to interpret, we can now explore the full linguistic potential of the text. We seek new rhythms in the words on the page, new emphases. We twist sentences out of shape just as Brooks did with the singsong lines of her poems. Perhaps, we even rearrange, change, and add to the words themselves. We decompose the words in order to recompose them into new forms. We become actors, who prepare roles by repeating their lines, trying various intonations in order to find odd riches in the script. If we listen to the syllables and play with the rhythm, the bare text suggests many directions the words could go in.

On this level, reading is a primal activity, not merely a rational derivative of writing. Reading occurs off center from our purposeful waking consciousness, then obtrudes into it. The text makes us aware of the stream of thoughts racing through us below the surface of our minds just as water flows silently through a creek bed until it strikes a boulder and starts to gurgle and splash. The text interferes with our stream of consciousness in such a way that it draws our attention. It alters our consciousness fundamentally. We do not go back to being the same people we were before we read it. All the properties of the text, including the purely physical and the phonological as well as the intellectual, shape who we are. Ideas eddy through our mind in queer ways. They acquire life force from the momentum of the stream. We could revolutionize our thinking about the world if we chose to follow the impetus of one of these ideas. We could change our whole life. In any case, our life does change, perhaps imperceptibly. The ideas we pick up from the act of reading become who we are. I don't mean the ideas intentionally conveyed via the text, which we grasp intellectually. I mean the ideas that the friction of the text spurred us to dream as we read it.

NOTES

1 Gwendolyn Brooks, "The Bean Eaters," *Selected Poems* (New York: Harper & Row, Publishers, 1963), p. 72.
2 Robert Creeley, "Was That a Real Poem or Did You Just Make It up Yourself?" in *Was That a Real Poem and Other Essays*, ed. Donald Allen (Bolinas, CA: Four Seasons Foundation, 1979), pp. 107–8.
3 Ralph Waldo Emerson, "Nature," in *Essays and Lectures*, ed. Joel Porte (New York: The Library of America, 1983), p. 7.
4 William James, *The Principles of Psychology*, vol. 1 (New York: Henry Holt and Company, 1890), pp. 609–10.
5 Ibid., pp. 606–7.

CHAPTER 3

The psychology of readers

A reader is self-composed of words. We readers consist of the words we experience in a text and the echoes they provoke in us. Words combine consciousness and the unconscious. Words do not point to or symbolize an unconscious that lies "inside" us out of direct reach. Words themselves are the unconscious in all its potency.

Let me dwell on the nature of the unconscious for a bit. People often imagine the unconscious as a kind of basement, with a solid floor and walls, that contains leftovers from our life we don't want anymore but somehow can't discard. Sigmund Freud believed that our basement consists of experiences from our personal past that we forgot or suppressed because they were traumatic. Freud argued that since the very young tend to have the same experiences, such as closeness to their mother and the discovery of mother and father having sex, people accumulate similar old furniture in their basements, most famously the Oedipus complex. These psychological patterns manifest themselves to our consciousness in the form of wish-fulfillment dreams or neuroses, such as compulsive hand-washing. When a neurosis disrupts our lives, the psychoanalyst helps us to revive the memory of the trauma at the root of the problem. Since our conscious mind knows how to distract us when we come near this memory, the psychoanalyst asks questions and listens for the telltale gaps in our testimony that indicate places where the trauma hides. Once we acknowledge the trauma, it ceases to disrupt our life.

C.G. Jung modified this image of the unconscious. Jung entered psychoanalysis with Freud and told him about the following dream:

> I was in a house I did not know, which had two stories. It was "my house." I found myself in the upper story where there was a kind of salon furnished in rococo style. On the

walls hung a number of precious paintings. I wondered that
this should be my house, and thought, "Not bad." But then
it occurred to me that I did not know what the lower floor
looked like. Descending the stairs, I reached the ground floor.
There everything was much older, and I realized that this part
of the house must date from about the fifteenth or sixteenth
century ... I came upon a heavy door, and opened it. Beyond
it, I discovered a stone stairway that led down into the cellar.
Descending again, I found myself in a beautifully vaulted room
which looked exceedingly ancient ... I knew that the walls
dated from Roman times. My interest was by now intense.
I looked more closely at the floor. It was one of stone slabs,
and in one of these I discovered a ring. When I pulled it, the
stone slab lifted, and again I saw a stairway of narrow stone
steps leading down into the depths. These, too, I descended,
and entered a low cave cut into the rock. Thick dust lay on
the floor, and in the dust were scattered bones and broken
pottery, like remains of a primitive culture.[1]

To explore the meaning of the dream, Jung turned to books:

The dream of the house had a curious effect upon me: it
revived my old interest in archaeology ... I took up a book on
Babylonian excavations, and read various works on myths. In
the course of this reading I came across Friedrich Creuzer's
The Symbolism and Mythology of Ancient Peoples—and that
fired me![2]

Freud wanted to interpret the dream according to his own theory
about the personal unconscious, but Jung thought it led more naturally
to this interpretation:

It was plain to me that the house represented a kind of image
of the psyche—that is to say, of my then state of consciousness, with hitherto unconscious additions. Consciousness
was represented by the salon. It had an inhabited atmosphere, in spite of its antiquated style.
    The ground floor stood for the first level of the uncon-
scious. The deeper I went, the more alien and the darker the
scene became. In the cave, I discovered remains of a primitive
culture, that is, the world of the primitive man within myself—a
world which can scarcely be reached or illuminated by

consciousness. The primitive psyche of man borders on the
life of the animal soul, just as the caves of prehistoric times
were usually inhabited by animals before men laid claim to
them.[3]

This dream helped Jung to formulate his theory of the collective unconscious. He envisioned the collective unconscious as a layer below
the personal unconscious that functions by generating symbols of universal significance, including art and myths. We all share in these basic symbols, according to Jung, not because we have gone through
similar experiences but because we have inherited them with our ge-
netic makeup. They are an innate part of being human, regardless of
personal history or culture just as Roman and prehistoric civilizations
form the heritage of all Western cultures.

Jung defined a small collection of patterns, or archetypes, that act
as lenses through which we make sense of the world: the shadow, the
anima, and the self. We encounter the archetypes through projection.
If we hate or fear someone, it's because we project onto others feelings
about the aspects of our own character we hate and fear yet don't want
to acknowledge. They become symbols of our shadow personality.
Likewise, when we fall in love, we project that part of our unconscious,
the soul or anima, onto others as well. Jung used the term "libido" to
describe this power of attraction. Libido does not necessarily require
sexual attraction. It encompasses intense friendships, devotion to ce-
lebrities, and other passionate attachments. Libido connects us mean-
ingfully to others. It binds individuals into societies. Its force drives
us to pay attention to those who are different from ourselves. Their
personalities, needs, and desires fascinate us. They become important
to us. We convert the energy of libido into the creativity and activities
necessary to build relationships with them.

We all participate in these symbols, said Jung, and they convey a
similar meaning to all of us. Hence, he referred to the "collective" unconscious. Nevertheless, we experience these archetypes as individuals.
Indeed, they help us to become a more individual self by granting each
of us access to capabilities we were unaware that we possessed. With
Jung, we still have discrete basements with solid walls, but the floor
now has a trap door leading to a network of catacombs that connect all
basements. The analytical psychologist guides us down into the catacombs to help us find the missing pieces we need to become a complete
self. Archetypes may erupt into our consciousness in the form of psy-
choses, their power sheering through the veneer of our waking personality. In that case, the psychologist helps us to convert the pathological

relationship between our ego and the dangerous archetype into a stable, useful one. In other cases, our waking self may lack a connection to the archetypes so that our life seems gray and unfulfilling. The psychologist shows us how to tap the creative power of the archetypes.

James Hillman, a post-Jungian psychologist, turned the basement metaphor inside out. Hillman pointed out that the soul/anima is more than a discrete symbol we carry around in our psyche. It is not a separable organ of the unconscious with a specific function; it is an instinct that shapes our whole engagement with the world:

> [The soul] desires to go beyond, to go ever inward and
> deeper. Why? This too [Heraclitus] answers, saying (frg. 54),
> "Invisible connection is stronger than visible." To arrive at
> the basic structure of things we must go into their darkness.
> Again, why? Because, says Heraclitus (frg. 123), "The real
> constitution of each thing is accustomed to hide itself ..."
> When we put together the few fragments we have just cited,
> we may realize that the depth dimension is the only one that
> can penetrate to what is hidden; and since only what is hidden
> is [the] true nature of all things, including nature itself, then
> only the way of the soul can lead to true insight. Heraclitus
> suggests that true equals deep, and he is opening the way for
> a psychological hermeneutic, a viewpoint of soul toward all
> things.[4]

The soul expresses itself through the metaphor of depth. We don't simply want to experience the world. We want to penetrate its secrets, know it intimately. The metaphor can play out in any number of ways. Going down in the basement of the unconscious is just one manifestation of the soul's instinct toward depth. Falling in love and becoming intimate with someone is another. Yet we can also love a landscape with the same intensity, as Hillman discovered on a trip to Japan:

> The wide world remains merely that, merely a place of es-
> cape or acting out, so long as the world "out the window" is
> imagined only in the Cartesian model as sheer *res extensa*
> [extended thing], only dead matter. To show more vividly
> how that world is, as Keats said, a place of soul, let us go
> straight through the window into the world. Let us take a walk
> in a Japanese garden, in particular the strolling garden, the
> one with water, hills, trees and flowers. While we walk, let us
> imagine the garden as an emblem for the peripatetic teacher

> or the therapeutic guide (psychopompos), *the world itself as
> psychoanalyst showing us soul,* showing us how to be in it
> soulfully.
>
>   I turn to the garden and to Japan because of insights given
> while in Kyoto gardens several years ago, and also because
> the garden as a metaphor expresses some of the deepest
> longings—for Hesperides, to Eden's paradise, and Maria's
> *hortus inclusus* [enclosed garden]—for the world as home of
> the soul. So, by entering into the Japanese garden now we
> shall be stepping through the window into the *anima mundi*
> [world's soul].[5]

Animals, plants, wild places, beautiful buildings… They can all attract us, draw us into their depths. We can love them as much as we love another person. The soul animates the whole world for us. When it is thus animated, the world becomes the soul. We enter the soul as into an environment and inhabit it. It is always all around us. Therefore, we don't need a trained psychologist anymore to help us find the soul. We just need to look at where we are right now in a soulful way.

Freud and Jung maintained the primacy of waking consciousness. They viewed psychology's job as associating the unconscious to the conscious mind. The very word unconscious indicates that consciousness forms its reference point. But things look different from the point of view of the unconscious. In a dream, Hillman says, our self shrinks in importance; it becomes one image among many:

> [T]he "I" in the dream is no secret stage director (Schopenhauer)
> who wrote the play he acts in, no self-portrait photographer
> taking his own snapshot from below, nor are the wants fulfilled
> in a dream the ego's wishes. The dream is not "mine," but the
> psyche's, and the dream-ego merely plays one of the roles in
> the theatre, subjected to what the "others" want, subject to the
> necessities staged by the dream.[6]

The images we encounter in our dreams often scare us because our self seems so frail, not the strong, individuated self that Jung envisions. As a result, the dream world lacks a center that consciousness typically gives things. The unconscious resembles the Hades into which Odysseus descends in the *Odyssey*, where the shades of the dead emerge from the darkness almost at random. The waking world would look like this as well except that consciousness imposes an apparent order on it. George Eliot imagined the world as a glass plate covered with random scratches. If we place a candle next to it, the scratches appear to form concentric circles around the flame. Our ego acts like the flame, organizing the innumerable stimuli of the world around its focus. This arbitrary viewpoint provides no more real a picture of the world than our dreams do. We could just as easily think of the dream world as real and the waking world as artificial.

Consciousness, then, becomes relative, not an absolute point of reference. When we are awake, we are conscious of certain things, unconscious of others. In waking life, people view the world empirically—we are sentient creatures while rocks are inanimate material that we perceive through physical sensation. When we are asleep, we are also conscious of certain things, unconscious of others. In dreams, every object feels significant—closer or farther from us but never inanimate. Even when we are awake, though, we can train ourselves to view the world the way we do in dreams. To do so, we must let go of the self-importance and officiousness of our interpreter, the ego, and acknowledge that every object in the world also conveys a feeling, not just physical stimuli. If we view the waking world as a dream, it becomes our unconscious. It differs from Jung's collective unconscious in that we do not filter the contents of our dream world only through archetypes that take a personal form (*our* shadow, *our* anima, *our* self). Instead, the world's objects remain impersonal, as much yours as mine.

If the waking world and the unconscious converge, we no longer need to descend into the underworld of dreams to find the soul. We don't need a psychologist to guide us in the dark. We don't need the specialized language of psychology to describe what we find. The soul manifests itself in the common objects around us, and we can determine their meaning for ourselves. We simply need to look at the world in a psychological manner. Words are objects in the world, too, and can, therefore, be the unconscious. The reader's self extends from out of the words just as it extends from out of the dream in Hillman's example. We would grasp this possibility if we stopped thinking of the text as a medium of communications and instead treated it as a garden to experience.

To see what I mean, let's go to ancient Greece and look at an early instance of the first-person narrator, dating from the sixth century B.C. As tombstones do today, the first Greek monuments employed the third person—"Here lies ..." The text serves as a label. It draws our attention to something without altering it. The text points to the contents of the grave, which we cannot see. We learn whose remains are buried in that spot through the mediation of the text. Our thought passes through the text, as through a window, to the corpse in the ground and the life that used to be attached to it. We don't fuss about how fully the inscription portrays the contents of the grave because all we care about is the grave, not the words. We only need them as a matter of convenience to say, "Here it is."

Then, monument carvers started using the first person. Writing from the perspective of "I" does alter the contents that the inscription supposedly describes. Consider this epigram attached to the statue of someone who died in childhood:

> As Phrasikleia's memorial, I will always be called girl since I received this lot from the gods instead of marriage.[7]

Certainly, the inscription locates the deceased and conveys information about her if that's what we want. However, the simple trick of writing in the first person performs the much more remarkable feat of animating the monument. The monument addresses us like any interlocutor. We face a three-dimensional personality. Although the inscription disarmingly acknowledges the difference between the statue and the actual Phrasikleia, the statue takes on Phrasikleia's characteristics. It is a girl just as she was, and it too once had, but lost, the potential for being married. The gods concern themselves with the fate of the statue in parallel with the fate of Phrasikleia. The statue even has as great a capacity for change and growth as Phrasikleia once had. The statue will "be called girl," a phrasing that implies it could, in fact, be other things if the gods so wished. "Girl" was not the statue's inevitable state and sole essence. It is merely a provisional identity, which could have changed if the gods had not decreed otherwise and frozen it in place.

"The gods" form the ground from which Phrasikleia's self springs. The inscription uses the indefinite plural deliberately, not specifying which particular gods determined Phrasikleia's lot. The text ascribes her self to the gods as a way of acknowledging its divine origin without being able to define it precisely just as we never know where our own linguistic creativity springs from. The self exhibits an articulate structure as though fashioned by a god. It's expressive. It conveys thought and feeling. But where that structure originates remains a mystery. Phrasikleia did not will it. The Greeks spoke of the gods the way we might speak of the imagination or the unconscious. The plurality of the gods leads inevitably to the many possibilities for Phrasikleia's self, of which "girl" forms one instance. One set of gods bestowed that identity. A different set would have given her another identity.

The first-person narration adds yet a further dimension to the life force of the statue. The ancient Greek visitor would have read the inscription aloud because silent reading had not been invented yet.

Throughout classical antiquity, people voiced the text in order to read it. We can imagine a visitor standing in front of Phrasikleia's monument as though meeting her for the first time. He sounds out the syllables to discover what they mean. The speech would seem spontaneous, of the moment. The reader would thus voice the role of the statue, reenacting its words as though he were an actor in a kind of miniature play who steps forward and delivers his line. In this way, the first-person inscription offers a mechanism for reviving Phrasikleia in the reader. The reader lends her a mouth, a tongue, a throat, and lungs. Indeed, a whole body belongs once again to Phrasikleia. The reader becomes Phrasikleia. "I" is not a character who happens to narrate the story. We ourselves become the character and inhabit the story. It becomes our self at least for the moment.

The self of the statue and inscription does not substitute for Phrasikleia's identity. It's not a matter of resemblance. The statue has generic features, and most visitors would never have seen the living Phrasikleia anyway. So the soul or force of the monument that they feel consists of something else beside the echo of the living girl it might have evoked for her family and friends. Indeed, they too never really knew Phrasikleia either, except as a self, that is, through the image or images she projected. As in a dream, all selves exist on the plane of image, regardless of whether they are "real" (the girl) or "fake" (the statue). The viewer or reader experiences them the same way and only subsequently do we attribute the self to life or art and assign different values to it.

The self comes from an act of linguistic creation. The Greeks and Romans imagined fate as an utterance. The gods observe humans and their actions dispassionately. At the critical moment, when the future of an individual hangs in the balance, the gods announce what will happen to him. The decree marks his character eternally. Hector will forever be known as the Trojan hero who was slain by Achilles and dragged around the walls of Troy behind a chariot. The gods made Hector's fate manifest by pronouncing it. The act of speaking this fate equals the fate itself. The word "fate" originally meant simply "that which has been said." What had seemed unclear and indeterminate to humans one moment becomes clear and fixed the next, after the gods speak. We readers fashion our own fates through a similar act of pronunciation. An undifferentiated stream of words flows swiftly before our eyes and through our minds. At some point, like Robert Creeley's student, we cease to be passive observers and become the protagonist of our own dreams. We pick out a passage that strikes us. We start to hear rhythms in the text. We create something new out of them. That is who we are. That is our fate.

NOTES

1 C.G. Jung, *Memories, Dreams, Reflections*, ed. Aniela Jaffe, trs. Richard and Clara Winston (New York: Vintage Books, 1989), pp. 158–9.
2 Ibid., p. 162.
3 Ibid., p. 160.
4 James Hillman, *The Dream and the Underworld* (New York: Harper & Row, Publishers, 1979), p. 26.
5 Hillman, "From Mirror to Window: Curing Psychoanalysis of Its Narcissism," *Spring: A Journal of Archetype and Culture* 49 (1989), p. 71.
6 Hillman, *The Dream and the Underworld*, pp. 102–3.
7 Jesper Svenbro, *Phrasikleia: An Anthopology of Reading in Ancient Greece*, tr. Janet Lloyd (Ithaca, NY and London: Cornell University Press, 1993), p. 17.

CHAPTER 4

Committing to the text

Nothing happens in reading unless we pay attention to the text. Reading is merely the form of attention we give to words. Attention, or consciousness, operates on many levels in reading as in any other part of our existence. The more we pay attention, the more meaning we derive from our experience. Reading can take the whole weight of our life if we need it to. The various forms and levels of attention translate into wholly different experiences for the reader, different echelons of meaning. Unfortunately, we often stick with just one layer or one type of meaning and never go further to uncover the riches that await our discovery. When we first start reading seriously, we are easily satisfied with the story or the information that the book conveys. Or we assume that only one kind of attention is appropriate in a given situation. We read one way at school, a different way in church. As a result, we invest less of ourselves in the text than we might—and create less meaning.

I learned just how much difference there can be between levels of attention from an embarrassing episode in college. In a class on Victorian literature, we studied Robert Browning's poetry. For the first class, the professor assigned "Count Gismond," a 126-line soliloquy from Browning's *Dramatic Lyrics*:

Count Gismond
Aix in Provence

I

Christ God who savest man, save most
  Of men Count Gismond who saved me!
Count Gauthier, when he chose his post,
  Chose time and place and company
To suit it; when he struck at length
My honour, 'twas with all his strength.

II

And doubtlessly ere he could draw
  All points to one, he must have schemed!
That miserable morning saw
  Few half so happy as I seemed,
While being dressed in queen's array
To give our tourney prize away.[1]

I read the poem for homework as did most of the other students. When I say "I read the poem," I mean I read the poem the way I read popular fiction at that time: Agatha Christie, Ian Fleming, J.R.R. Tolkien, and so on. It took 10 minutes to read "Count Gismond."

The professor started class with a preamble on Browning and then asked us what the themes of "Count Gismond" were. No one answered. She phrased the question another way. Again, no answer. She reformulated her question to spark our minds, with no better results. Then, she asked us to repeat the bare details of setting and characters. She must have seen from our blank faces that it was hopeless. For myself, I could not remember a thing about the poem. All details had evaporated from my memory. After 15 minutes, the professor gave up. "I want you to go back and read the poem again," she said emphatically. "Don't just pass your eyes over the words. You have to actually *read* it." She dismissed us for the day.

I realized that she was asking us to devote an attention to the text I had never given words before. So right after the dressing down from my professor, I went to a study hall on campus and found a carrel next to a window with the January sun glaring in. I opened my Norton Critical Edition of *Robert Browning's Poetry*—I have the very volume next to me now—to page 59, where "Count Gismond" starts. I flattened the book on the desk (the spine is broken in that place). I rested both elbows on the edge of the desk and hunched my shoulders over the book. I read with my mind unnaturally tensed. I struggled through the poem, stanza by stanza, constantly looking at the line numbers to see how far I had gotten and how far I still had to go. I read each line slowly and with all the attention I could muster.

The stilted sentences exhausted me. I had to read twice or three times to understand them. Who says "Christ God?" You say Christ or God, but not the two together. Who uses the same word three times in one short sentence—"savest," "save," "saved?" Why did Browning or the speaker of the poem use an inverted construction—"save most/of men Count Gismond"? Shouldn't it read "most of all, save Count Gismond"? I didn't believe that Browning needed to torture the language like this to fit his meter and rhyme scheme. I assumed he employed the odd syntax and word choices to make the poem sound old-fashioned, but that didn't seem a complete explanation. All these questions with no obvious answers, and I had just read two lines!

In a Browning soliloquy, the speaker assumes a knowledge of circumstances which the reader does not possess. The speaker talks as if to a confidant or at least someone who knows the events and personalities that the soliloquy refers to. The reader, privy to none of this, just happens to "overhear" the speech. Therefore, he must read between the lines to understand the background. For example, we do not learn that the speaker of "Count Gismond" is a woman till line 11, and even then the poem implies it rather than stating it outright—the speaker says she "dressed in queen's array." Except, Browning doesn't even state it that directly. He says, "That miserable morning saw/Few half so happy as I seemed,/While being dressed in queen's array/to give our tourney prize away." I was so busy figuring out what "Few half so happy" meant (it makes sense if you mentally insert a "who were" after "Few") that I missed the fact that the participial phrase ("While being …") must refer to the speaker. I struggled through circumlocutions ("he struck at length/my honour"—how was I supposed to know what this meant if I didn't even know who was saying it?) and ambiguity ("That miserable morning saw/Few half so happy as I *seemed*"—was she happy in fact or did she only appear so?).

Browning expects us to pay close attention to his language, for there lies the drama. The verbal tics reveal the psychology of the speaker: the hesitations, the grandiosity, the self-consciousness, the subjective coloring given to the action, the shading of facts, and the concealments. Each small placement of a word or line break adds a delicate note to what builds into a symphony. Nothing in the poem exists by chance or for mere convenience. Thus, the only way I could understand "Count Gismond" was by main force, rereading sentence by sentence to pry open their literal meaning and then piecing together the situation and motives of the speaker. She is young and appears in public on her birthday to be crowned queen. Two young cousins appear with her, who could be rivals for the throne:

> They, too, so beauteous! Each a queen
>   By virtue of her brow and breast;
> Not needing to be crowned, I mean,
>   As I do.

(19–22)

The interjection after the semicolon reveals her anxiety. She can't help reminding the listener who the real queen is, yet the almost involuntary choice of "queen" to describe the cousins admits their qualification for the throne. The moment has come for her to award the prize to the victor of the joust:

> But Gauthier, and he thundered "Stay!"
> And all stayed. "Bring no crowns, I say!
>
> "Bring torches! Wind the penance-sheet
>   About her! Let her shun the chaste,
> Or lay herself before their feet!
>   Shall she whose body I embraced
> A night long, queen it in the day?
> For honour's sake no crowns, I say!"
>
> (53–60)

Gauthier interrupts the public ceremony of crowning the victor because he calls into question the queen's fitness for this office and by implication for the throne itself. To dramatize her disgrace, he wants her to do public penance for the adultery they had committed together in the past. Adulterous women were made to wear a white sheet and to bare their head, arms, and legs. Gauthier's accusation threatens her position. If he were her lover, why did he make it? Had she dumped him? Had he repented of the sin himself? Was it an attempted coup? We never receive a hint about his motivation because the speaker of the poem, the queen, only thinks about her own concerns. She can't utter a word in her own defense—is it because she is dumbfounded by Gauthier's audacity or because she knows he can prove her guilt? The situation hangs in doubt until Gismond challenges and kills Gauthier. She expresses no regret or horror at his death, just relief and triumph. She relates his dying words, which retract the accusation. Do we take them at face value, or has she put them in his mouth to dispel any doubt about her own chastity? Gismond took her for his wife—was this before or after the tournament? She bears children—but whose are they? The ambiguities in the queen's account and the choices she makes in telling her own story reveal her character, with all its complexities.

I had discovered the riches that the analysis of books can yield. I couldn't have found those ideas about "Count Gismond" simply by passing the words in front of my eyes. I learned how to ask questions of a text systematically. Who is the speaker? What is her situation?

What choices does she make? And so on. Literary criticism is a research discipline like physics, economics, or archeology, and any discipline imposes constraints. We gather evidence, chiefly the text. We can propose any interpretation we like as long as we support it with evidence. Ideally, the interpretation takes the form of a model that applies more broadly to the author's work or to all works of a certain kind. The model should have explanatory power so that it yields new insight when applied to texts other than the one that inspired it. We must follow certain rules when we use our model to explicate the text. We look for ambiguity and all the other tricks and tools of the poet, but we cannot pretend an ambiguity that we can't demonstrate objectively. We can study the historical period in which the poem is set as well as the context in which it was composed, but we must limit ourselves only to what the author could have known and experienced. We can apply feminist, psychological, or other theories as long as they don't make anachronistic assumptions but instead elucidate human structures that existed in the author's time. Also, we cannot inject our own personal concerns into the text any more than a judge can decide cases based on his own private opinions.

All of these restrictions aim to ensure that any interpretation reflects the objective meaning of the text. Like a careful forensic pathologist, the reader has not contaminated the sample with foreign matter. But this objectivity limits the effect that critical reading can have on us. In the Victorian Lit class, my interpretations of the texts meant nothing to me personally apart from the transient thrill of working out a puzzle. Reading became a kind of game to see which of us could come up with the richest ideas within the rules of the discipline. I spent the rest of the semester honing my playing skills. For a time, I enjoyed impressing the professor or throwing out ideas that reoriented class discussion. If I had continued, I could have earned straight A's in the rest of my literature classes and gone off to a top graduate school for my Ph.D. in English. This analytical work would not have changed who I am. I would not have become a richer person. So the profession of literature did not seem as serious, as risky, as adventurous as I wished. Disenchanted, I dropped out of the Victorian Lit class in the second semester and vowed to look for professors and literature that fed my soul.

We can connect to literature emotionally just as intensely as we can intellectually although we bring a different set of eyes to the text and derive different values from it. The aesthetics of reading change. Emotional readers become personally invested in the book. It becomes part of our life. We do not judge what the book should or might mean to somebody as a critical reader would. We believe that it does mean something to us and that we must work, struggle, and alter our way of thinking—even change ourselves if necessary—in order to align ourselves with what that meaning is. We don't grade the text down if it lacks writerly virtues such as Browning's economy with words. Instead, we look to understand the beauty and insight we know is there, however the text is written.

The *Koran* presupposes a different relationship to books than modern literary study. Someone trained to read by modern methods notices the lack of economy when the *Koran* repeats a passage. Here, from the surah "Pilgrimage," God tells Muhammad what to think if the people resist his message:

> If they deny you, remember that before them the peoples of Noah, of Abraham and of Lot, the tribes of Thamud and 'Ad, and the dwellers of Midian had denied their apostles: Moses was also rejected. I bore long with the unbelievers, and then My scourge overtook them. How dire was the way I rejected them!
>
> [22:42ff][2]

In "Repentance," God calls out the wealthier, mightier people from the past whose "works in this life" were "vain":

> Have they not heard the histories of those who have gone before them? The fate of Noah's people and of Thamud and 'Ad; of Abraham's people and the people of Midian and the Ruined Cities? Their apostles showed them veritable signs. God did not wrong them, but they wronged themselves.
>
> [9:70][3]

In "Al-Furqan":

> As for Noah's people, We drowned them when they denied their apostles and made of them an example to all men. For the wrongdoers We have prepared a woeful scourge.
>
> The tribes of Thamud and 'Ad were also destroyed, and so were those who dwelt at Rass, and many generations in between. To each of them We gave examples, and each of them We exterminated.
>
> [25:38–9][4]

In "The Spider":

> And to the people of Midian We sent their compatriot Shu'aib.
> He said: "Serve God, my people. Look forward to the Last
> Day. Do not corrupt the earth with wickedness."
>   But they denied him. The earth shook beneath their
> feet, and when morning came they were prostrate in their
> dwellings.
>   'Ad and Thamud We also destroyed. This is vouchsafed
> for by their ruins. Satan had made their foul deeds seem fair
> to them and debarred them from the right path, keen-sighted
> though they were.
>
> [29:36–8][5]

In fact, the *Koran* cites Thamud and 'Ad to make this sort of point about two dozen times. The modern reader finds such repetition odd, archaic, a sign of unsophisticated writing and unsystematic thinking. A modern writer does not need to repeat a fact once, let alone dozens of times, to get the point across. He expects readers to notice and remember the first time. Modern readers also want to find out who or what Thamud and 'Ad are. We assume the writer wrote in a specific time and place and that he alluded to events which, if not historically accurate, at least were vivid in the minds of his contemporaries. We search for the deeper point that has been lost across time and culture.

Emotional readers need no special methods to find the meaning. The very fact that we do not know Thamud and 'Ad illustrates how thoroughly they have been destroyed. These places or people once existed, and now no one even remembers their name. If we do not believe that God destroyed them, we at least appreciate that destruction does come upon human societies. We learn what complete destruction means from the perspective of elapsed centuries. The repetition of this example drives home the point that we cannot escape the potential for destruction any more than we can avoid running across "Thamud and 'Ad" in the *Koran*. It always looms over us.

The repetition serves another purpose, too. Instead of making a philosophical argument about the meaning of Thamud and 'Ad, the brief, periodic mentions drip-feed ideas to us. Here, we learn God had sent apostles to Thamud and 'Ad. There, we learn the apostles had shown signs to Thamud and 'Ad. Elsewhere, we learn Thamud and 'Ad had examples to learn from in their time just as we have *them* as examples in ours. In another place, we learn Satan confused Thamud and 'Ad about good and bad deeds, and so on. The *Koran* proceeds by insinuating tiny thought after tiny thought about Thamud and 'Ad. None of them rise to the level of statements that demand corroboration and critical inquiry. They slip into our mind as possibilities. What happened to Thamud and 'Ad could happen to us. Therefore, we respond to the text by reflecting, "What if there were apostles at Thamud and 'Ad? Who were they?" We then think, "What if there are apostles here today? Who are they?" We apply the text directly to our lives.

As we read, we add this possibility to that possibility so that over the course of the *Koran*, a new way of conceiving the world takes root in our mind without our fully realizing it. We see patterns that we didn't see before. Our individual and collective fate is bound intricately to our actions. It is not left to chance. The big things happen for a reason. We contribute to that reason by what we choose to do. If we choose to do the right things, we can live happily. If not, we hasten the destruction of ourselves and those around us. The diffuseness of the text—the very nonwriterly qualities of its style—enables these ideas to evade the censor of our critical faculties. The style of the *Koran* discourages our intelligence from playing games. We don't interpret the text as though it doesn't pertain to us. We read "Count Gismond" implicitly in the past tense because critical readers can't detach the poem from the historical circumstances in which Browning wrote it. We read the *Koran* in the present tense because we let it speak to us.

The historian of Islam Marshall G.S. Hodgson notes, "Many non–Muslims have found [the *Koran*] a jumbled and incoherent mass, ridden with repetitions, and have been at a loss to fathom why Muslims regard it as supremely beautiful."[6] For readers who allow the *Koran* to shape their lives, the frequent appearance of "Thamud and 'Ad, and the dwellers of Midian" doesn't sound wearisome or threatening as Hodgson explains:

> The *Koran* must not be read through but rather must be participated in: it must be recited, as an act of self-dedication and of worship. The *Koran* presents at every point one great challenge: to accept the undertaking of faith. To recite it truly is to be accepting and affirming that undertaking. Then its beauty can be responded to line by line and one will delight in the juxtaposition, whatever the immediate subject, of all its main themes within any given passage. The repetitious phrases remind one of the total context in which a given passage must be understood: in even a small part of the *Koran*, the act of worship can be complete.[7]

The *Koran* combines features of oral tradition with written literature. The syntax and rhetorical patterns are simple and are repeated frequently. Repetitions characterize oral performance as the storyteller needs a set of stock phrases and passages that he can throw in at any point to keep the narration going for the audience while he prepares the next original idea in his mind. Thamud and 'Ad offer a standard illustration about people in the past who ignored the apostles sent to them, and the idea is general enough that it can fit plausibly in many places. A speaker can use it within discussions of any number of larger themes: the nature of faith, the conduct of the faithful in war, the promise of heaven, and so on. But the *Koran* doesn't repeat these Thamud and 'Ad passages with identical wording as a purely oral poet or preacher would. A writer has added different details to stamp each instance with its own emphasis. Each one advances the argument a little bit. Thus, the *Koran* has been written and is meant to be read yet with some of the conditions of oral performance. The word *Koran* means "recitation." The *Koran* represents the transcript of a recitation in live voice. Muhammad wrote down the *Koran* at the dictation of the archangel Gabriel, who had been sent by God. Muhammad used to go to a cave in a mountain north of Mecca to meditate, and there, in 610, Gabriel first appeared to him as described in "The Star":

> By the declining star, your compatriot [Muhammad] is not in error, nor is he deceived!
>
> He does not speak out of his own fancy. This is an inspired revelation. He is taught by one [Gabriel] who is powerful and mighty.
>
> He stood on the uppermost horizon; then, drawing near, he came down within two bows' length or even closer, and revealed to his servant that which he revealed.
>
> His own heart did not deny his vision. How can you, then, question what he sees?
>
> [53:1–8][8]

Gabriel did not simply preach while Muhammad listened passively and mechanically inscribed the words on paper. Mohammed had to repeat the words in his turn. In "Clots of Blood," Gabriel exhorts Muhammad:

> Recite in the name of your lord who created—created man from clots of blood.
>
> Recite! Your Lord is the Most Bountiful One, who by the pen taught man what he did not know.
>
> [96:1–2][9]

I said that Gabriel utters the preceding passage, but I could just as well have said that Muhammad does. For Muhammad assumed the role of Gabriel toward us when he turned the archangel's spoken words into a text, and we readers must listen, learn, and recite the verses of the *Koran* just as Muhammad did. It's not enough to let the words pass silently through our minds. We must reenact Muhammad's original encounter with Gabriel by reciting them. The *Koran* does not offer a mere text; it also tells us how to read it. In "The Cow," passages often begin this way:

> Say: "Whoever is an enemy of Gabriel" (who has by God's grace revealed to you the Koran as a guide and joyful tidings for the faithful, confirming previous scriptures) "whoever is an enemy of God, His angels, or His apostles, or Gabriel or Michael, will surely find that God is the enemy of the unbelievers."
>
> [1:97–98][10]

"Say" it. To truly read the *Koran*, we must speak the words, whether aloud or in our head, so that the sound resonates inside us. The text becomes a palpable experience as though it were a face-to-face encounter with another being. By reciting, we cease to be detached observers and become participants in the cosmic drama.

Readers from the beginning helped to enact the *Koran*'s meaning in the world: "the human impact of the *Koran* as a sheer piece of writing is undeniable," says Hodgson.[11] The book galvanized Arabs into conquering the Middle East and North Africa within a generation or two. They then created a vast new society based on the teachings of the *Koran*:

> The *Koran* spoke not only in the language of but to the personal and social needs of a particular group of Arabians, of Meccans and Medinese, with particular social and moral problems. By their responses, positive and negative, they built concrete meaning into what might otherwise have remained on the verbal level as general exhortations and observations. Without such response, which indeed is presupposed in the later portions of the *Koran* itself, it could at most have become a striking but otherwise inconsequential piece of literature.[12]

The theology and culture that developed out of the *Koran* represent one set of meanings that have given purpose and value to people's lives. However, those who engage in participatory reading of the *Koran* today do not have to accept the machinery of Islam anymore than we have to become Jews or Christians if we read the Bible with feeling. This method of reading the *Koran* or any book does not predetermine the meaning we find in it. We can commit ourselves to a text without tying ourselves to the traditions and institutions that have grown up around it in other times and places. Emotional commitment still leaves us free. We can plumb the text just as critical readers do. We can use our creativity to find our own meanings and give more value to our lives in our own way.

There is yet a third mode of attention, imaginative reading. The imaginative reader reenacts the text in his mind. William Blake's *Jerusalem*, his last work completed just 15 years before Browning's *Dramatic Lyrics*, places similar demands on the reader's critical faculties. *Jerusalem* offers an intricate, idiosyncratic mythology and a peculiar language to go along with it. We must read the text closely to untangle them. We probably also need to read Blake's earlier prophetic works, where he developed this mythology, to fully grasp his mythological framework.

When we start to understand *Jerusalem*—or any of Blake's works— we realize that he expects us to *live* the myths he has created. The people and things we encounter in the world are the organs of our soul. "Thirteen years ago. I lost a brother," Blake writes in a letter, "& with his spirit I converse daily & hourly in the Spirit. & See him in my re-membrance in the regions of my Imagination. I hear his advice & even now write from his Dictation."[13] Blake isn't expressing hyperbolic grief; he's describing his creativity matter-of-factly—it comes literally from his brother's spirit. Nor is the soul populated just by images of real people. Blake was a painter and engraver, and he wrote a description for a catalog of one of his pictures, "A Vision of the Last Judgment." Biblical figures populate the image:

> it ought to be understood that the Persons Moses & Abraham
> are not here meant but the States Signified by those Names
> the Individuals being representatives of Visions of those
> States as they were revealed to Mortal Man in the Series of
> Divine Revelations.[14]

All of the figures in Blake's poetry and art represent universal states and faculties of the human soul. They belong to the reader as well as to the poet. Blake wants us to reflect on what is the Moses in us, what is the Abraham.

More than that, Blake wants us to use the awareness of our soul, which he gives us, to change ourselves. He wants us to expand our minds so that we too become creative. He views us as slumbering, shrunken caricatures of the godlike people we were meant to be. We can become only so stupid and selfish before the process reverses:

> There is a limit of Opakeness, and a limit of Contraction;
> In every Individual Man, and the limit of Opakeness,
> Is named Satan: and the limit of Contraction is named Adam.
> But when Man sleeps in Beulah, the Saviour in mercy takes
> Contractions Limit, and of the Limit he forms Woman: That
> Himself may in process of time be born Man to redeem
> But there is no Limit of Expansion! there is no Limit of
>   Translucence.
> In the bosom of Man for ever from eternity to eternity.[15]

We may not understand what Blake means by limitless expansion and translucence, but he has presented a clear choice: look for the unrealized potentiality of our soul or ignore Blake altogether. Readers must engage with Blake's text the way he exhorts us to do or walk away from it. He offers no good-faith alternative. If we accept his drama of the soul as real, we must strive to expand ourselves according to the directions he gives. If we don't accept this premise, the text contains merely the eccentric fantasies of a long-dead poet, and we waste our time to read it because it barely connects to anything in the familiar world. "Count Gismond" hones our ability to analyze psychology. The *Koran* encourages us to consider the relationship between our behavior and the state of the world. Thus, these works can lead us out of the book and into the world. The figures and events in *Jerusalem* refer entirely to what happens within ourselves. Satan, Adam, and the other Biblical names that Blake invokes represent the states and faculties of our own inner selves. We don't need to know about the Bible to understand what Blake means; we just need to reflect on the Satan and the Adam inside us. "Mark well my words! they are of your eternal salvation," Blake says in *Milton*.[16] In other words, your soul is at stake. Either we take the challenge personally or we become mere gawkers at the weird furniture in a strange poet's mind. We must personally involve ourselves in the text. Otherwise, reading Blake is foolish.

Blake's multilayered epic *Jerusalem* describes the restoration of the heavenly Jerusalem. In the poem, Jerusalem is both a female figure and the image of a city or community—the ideal toward which the inhabitants of an actual city such as Blake's own London unconsciously aspire. For the individual, Jerusalem is the soul, or as Blake puts it in his subtitle, *The Emanation of The Giant Albion*. Albion, a male figure, stands for England, and each English person could become an Albion or an ideal representative of the nation if he enlarges his mind. An analytical

psychologist today would use the term "projection" rather than emanation to describe Jerusalem's relationship to Albion. Jerusalem represents
an image that articulates an otherwise unconscious idea that Albion/
England/Englishmen need to realize about themselves.

The poem begins with Jerusalem and Albion falling into a deep sleep
(symbolizing Albion losing touch with the soul), and the bulk of the poem
describes an elaborate mythological machinery by which Jerusalem is res-
urrected and Albion reawakens. Albion has four "Zoas," which correspond
to the four faculties of analytical psychology: intellect, feeling, sensuality,
and intuition. The Zoas are double figures. Each appears in his "risen" or
waking state as well as in his "fallen" or sleeping state. Urizen (your reason) is the Zoa of intellect, who appears in his fallen state as Satan. Luvah
(lover) is the Zoa of emotion; Orc is his fallen state. Thamas (possibly from
the Greek *thauma*, marvel) is the Zoa of the senses, and his fallen state is
Adam. Urthona (earth owner) is the Zoa of imagination, whose fallen
state is Los. The risen figures are godlike while the fallen figures bear a de-
monic resemblance to them—they symbolize our psychopathology. Each
risen Zoa has its own female emanation as does each fallen Zoa. When
Albion falls asleep, so do all the risen Zoas. Consequently, the fallen Zoas
become dominant. *Jerusalem* describes the intricate process by which the
four risen Zoas and their emanations are revived one by one. The mutual
love of the Zoas and their emanations rouses the risen figures from their
sleep. When they have all awakened, Albion and Jerusalem awaken. Man
has recovered the full capabilities of his soul.

Urthona/Los drives the process. He represents human creativity,
especially poets and other artists. Blake depicts this Zoa as a blacksmith
who resurrects a fallen world by beating time with his hammer and
anvil. These rhythmic hammer blows forge links in a chain. Think of
the links as precise intervals of space and time that take concrete form
(duration blocks). In the fallen, empirical world, time and space appear
random and empty. In physics, every segment of time and space is
like every other segment. They can be filled with anything. A square
yard in the city measures the same as a square yard in the country. An
hour spent at work lasts just as long as an hour on vacation. I happen
to occupy this space at this time, but someone else could just as easily
have done so. I perform a series of activities during my day, but I could
have performed them in a different order or chosen different activities
altogether. Physics can explain why we occupy this space at this time
only by pointing to the preceding events that maneuvered us into this
position—I am the inevitable result of the blind interaction of matter
going back to the beginning of the universe. Therefore, no particular
meaning attaches to our being here rather than there. If time and space

are random, so must the life be of those who occupy it. My life has no inherent meaning.

Blake wanted to restore meaning to our relationship with the world. Urthona's chain represents the *necessity* of the passage of moments. The moments do not occur at random; rather, each link or moment must occur at a specific interval and in a specific form to fulfill a larger pattern of experience. Rhythm provides a definitive answer to the question of why something happens in a particular time and place. A rhythm or pattern dictates what each of its elements is and the order in which they all occur. The elements must occur in a specific order to complete the rhythm. J.S. Bach once wrote part of a concerto and handed it to a colleague to finish. "You can see how the rest of this goes," Bach said. Once a composer has established the rhythm, necessity compels the rest of the elements to fall into place. The musician doesn't play notes at random or rush through them as fast as he can for expedience. He plays the specific notes that the composition demands, and he plays them in time with the beat. For Blake, the poet or artist restores meaning to the world by creating or making manifest a rhythm into which our consciousness and our lives fit and to which they contribute. Our participation recovers a beautiful form for the world. The world and I become necessary to each other, linked by the chain of rhythm, no longer chance acquaintances.

In *Jerusalem*, the breakthrough comes in the last section, chapter 4, when Urthona starts the work of pounding out the cosmic rhythm with his hammer. The links Urthona forges make each segment of the world necessary or meaningful, and this reality eventually revives Jerusalem just as a melody emerges from the discrete notes that a musician plays.

Blake does not simply write *about* necessity in *Jerusalem*. His verse literally becomes the chain of necessity that Urthona forges. Instead of links or hammer blows, Blake creates his rhythm out of syllables. However, he rejects the regularity that most English verse follows, especially the ten-syllable, five-stress iambic pentameter line, found in Shakespeare and Milton. Such a metrical scheme would be just as arbitrary as the intervals of time and space in physics. Instead, Blake arranges the syllables in an organic prosody whose lines vary in length (mostly between 13 and 17 syllables) according to the ideas they express. Blake explains in his introduction to the poem:

> When this verse was first dictated to me I consider'd a Monotonous Cadence like that used by Milton & Shakspeare & all writers of English Blank Verse, derived from the modern bondage of rhyming; to be a necessary and indispensable part of Verse. But I soon found that in the mouth of a true

> Orator such monotony was not only awkward, but as much a
> bondage as rhyme itself. I have therefore produced a variety
> in every line, both of cadences & number of syllables. Every
> word and every letter is studied and put into its fit place: the
> terrific numbers are reserved for the terrific parts—the mild &
> gentle, for the mild & gentle parts, and the prosaic for inferior
> parts: all are necessary to each other.[17]

Notice that, much as Muhammad does, Blake conceives himself simply as writing down verses that a spirit dictated to him—no arbitrary human creation here but the reproduction of a divine realm. Blake has constructed *Jerusalem* with extraordinary precision, each tiny element finding its proper place. Ultimately, these elements build together into a whole, coherent epic.

The poem *Jerusalem* provides a kind of map that enables the reader to get back in touch with his soul. As Blake puts it at the end of chapter 3, in anticipation of Jerusalem's restoration in the following chapter:

> I give you the end of a golden string,
>   Only wind it into a ball:
> It will lead you in at Heavens gate,
>   Built in Jerusalem's wall.[18]

The string symbolizes both the flow of Blake's verse and the flow of the reader's consciousness. The string is thus another permutation of Urthona's chain. The action carried on by the mythological figures of the poem projects the experience that the reader should have when he follows the rhythm of Blake's text.

In my last year as an undergraduate, I read Blake as an independent study. I read Blake's prophetic works through as well as I could, but I still couldn't quite grasp the structure and purpose of his mythology. I went to the library one morning to read *Jerusalem* for a second time. I found a deserted corner on the fourth floor. I sat down at a round table, pulled up a comfortable chair, and opened the book flat on the table top. I read slowly and intently much as I had read "Count Gismond" a few years earlier. I muscled my way through chapters 1 and 2. The effort paid off. I finally grasped who all the figures were and what they symbolized. The confusing plot started to make sense. I had buried myself so intently in the text that I lost track of time.

I got up and took a spin around the fourth floor to stretch my legs. I sat back down to read chapters 3 and 4. As I read, I became more aware of the rhythms of Blake's verse. I followed it line by line, irregular though the lines of his poetry are. My eyes and mind could have pushed ahead faster if I had wanted only to decode the words, but I forced myself to keep to the pace of Blake's rhythm. I read no faster than the syllables wanted to come. I experienced the text as two simultaneous streams. I understood the syntax, with the usual stress contours of English which accentuate the meaning of the words. At the same time, the verse flowed in patterns of long and short vowels, which sometimes emphasized the same and sometimes different syllables. The denotative and prosodic strands intertwined polyphonically. When I got to chapter 4, far from growing tired, I experienced a kind of relaxed lucidity. The rhythms and the unfolding story seemed strangely to coincide. The rhythms of my mind had slowed to the same cadence. I no longer observed the story impatiently from the outside but belonged to it. It was going on within me, or I was going on within it.

By the time I reached the end, I was filled with a distinct, generalized feeling of love. I recognized it as the love that the Zoas and their emanations felt for each other, the mutual love of Albion and Jerusalem. I closed the book, rose from my seat, and slowly made my way back downstairs and out of the library. It was now late in the afternoon, the rhythms of Blake's verse still ran through my mind. Everything I saw looked the same as when I had entered, but things stood out more intensely—the institutional furniture, the gray carpeting, the row upon row of tan metal bookshelves, the irregular lines of books, each with a white square low on the spine where the call number is, the concrete staircase, its steps polished by the numerous people who had climbed them, white desks at circulation, the thin gateway and metal bar at the entrance, the hexagonal asphalt paving blocks in the quad, the white concrete sidewalks, the green grass and newly planted trees, the blacktop and ranks of cars in the parking lot. The ordinary objects of my environment had acquired new beauty, became somehow more meaningful. I felt that I belonged there among them at that moment. I realized that my soul had come alive to renew the world for me. The rhythm of Blake's poem had accomplished in me the very object of Blake's story. My own Jerusalem had reawakened.

My experience with *Jerusalem* struck me as so profound that I decided to go to graduate school to study how the rhythms of poetry alter a reader's consciousness. I spent the next five years pursuing this work. Reading Blake had liberated tremendous mental energy in me. I read experimental poetry. I studied psychology, prosody, phonology, and poetics. I wrote a thesis proposing a theory of prosody for modern free verse. Reading, and that day's reading in particular, changed my life.

Strange as it may seem, the esoteric knowledge I pursued led me out into the wider world. The experience of soul in one small domain gives us leverage everywhere else. We can relate to any new domain by looking at it soulfully. Phenomena that before seemed only dry and utilitarian now reveal depths of interest. They become animate. They draw us to them. They sprout possibilities. We want to learn more, develop a more intimate relationship with them. In my case, I ended up writing research for a company that advises corporations, governments, and nonprofits about the business uses of information technology. I discovered that the flexible, pragmatic ethos of business better suits the looser methods of reading that interest me than an academic discipline.

I write about personal involvement with the text, but I am really talking about the way we attach ourselves to the world.

NOTES

1 Robert Browning, *Robert Browning's Poetry*, ed. James F. Loucks (New York and London: W.W. Norton & Co., 1979), p. 59.
2 *The Koran*, tr. N.J. Dawood (London: Penguin Books, 1990) p. 238.
3 Ibid., p. 140.
4 Ibid., p. 255.
5 Ibid., p. 281.
6 Marshall G.S. Hodgson, *The Venture of Islam*, vol. 1, *The Classical Age of Islam* (Chicago: The University of Chicago Press, 1974), p. 184.
7 Ibid., p. 184.
8 *Koran.*, pp. 371–2.
9 Ibid., p. 429.
10 Ibid., p. 19.
11 Hodgson., p. 80.
12 Ibid., pp. 80–81.
13 William Blake, *The Complete Poetry & Prose of William Blake*, ed. David V. Erdman (Garden City, New York: Anchor Books, 1982), p. 705.
14 Ibid., p. 556.
15 Ibid., p. 189.
16 Ibid., p. 100.
17 Ibid., p. 145f.
18 Ibid., p. 231.

CHAPTER 5

The archetypes of meaning

The deepest meaning lulls us. We enter it. We luxuriate in it. And we never leave to go somewhere else. It blinds us to other possibilities in the world.

I learned this lesson while finishing a degree in Classics one summer. The Classics faculty at my university generously agreed to teach me one on one. Ronald Zirin took me through my first Greek tragedy, Euripides' *The Bacchae*. The play appealed to him because he himself was studying for a second Ph.D. in psychology. Euripides seemed quite modern to the twentieth century because of his depiction of psychological complexes, above all in *The Bacchae*. Zirin chose an annotated edition of the play, with introduction by E.R. Dodds. Dodds later expanded the introduction into *The Greeks and the Irrational* (1951) about the treatment of irrational psychological impulses in ancient Greek art and religion.

Every night, I would pick my way laboriously through 100 lines of the play. The next morning I would appear at Zirin's office. He had thin black hair, drank coffee, and kept a toothpick in his mouth most of the time. I would spend the hour translating the passages I had worked up. He corrected my mistakes and helped me over the rough spots. Occasionally, he would pause to fill me in about the structure of Greek tragedies, versification, Euripides as an author, the historical background of the play, and so on. But our most interesting discussions revolved around psychology. I had read a lot of C.G. Jung, who had made a study of psychosis and its relationship to mythology. So we had a common language to talk about the play.

The Bacchae deals most directly with the irrational of any Greek tragedy. The play depicts the apotheosis of Dionysos, or Bacchus, the god of wine, revelry, and earthy impulses. It starts with the arrival of Dionysos in Greece. He had introduced his cult first in Asia and made his way West in a march of conquest until he came to the city of Thebes. The Theban women, including the mother and the aunts (Ino and Agave) of the young king Pentheus, don fawn skins and go out into the fields to perform the god's ceremonies. The elderly prophet Tiresias and Cadmus (the former king and Pentheus' grand-father) participate as well. The whole state threatens to convert to the worship of a foreign god. In one of the rituals, these Bacchae chase wild animals through the fields, rip them apart with their bare hands, and eat the flesh raw. Back in Thebes, Pentheus denies that Dionysos is really a god. He suspects Dionysos merely offers an excuse for women to engage in orgies. He sets out to suppress the worship of Dionysos and restore order. Consequently, he arrests and throws into the palace dungeon a follower of Dionysos, who is actually Dionysos in disguise. Dionysos destroys the palace by earthquake and fire. The "follower" escapes and describes the incident to the chorus of Bacchants:

CHORUS: Didn't he even grab hold of your hands in fetter-like nooses?
DIONYSOS: These things also outraged him, since he seemed to bind me
            But didn't graze nor grab us yet nourished his hope.
            Seeing a bull at the manger where he dragged us and shut us up,
            He threw nooses around its knees and hoofs—
            He was breathing hard, dropping sweat from his body,
            His teeth showing between his lips. And I was right there beside him,
            And I sat calmly and watched.

                                                          (615–22)

The scene illustrates the futility of a mortal trying to wrestle down the bull-like power of a god. Pentheus misdirects his force onto a delusive object, the bull, while the untouched god looks on.

Subsequently, the escaped follower/Dionysos persuades Pentheus to go out into the fields undercover to find out what is happening so that he can take action more effectively. Pentheus readily agrees and dresses up in fawn skins as a female Bacchant. Dionysos causes Pentheus' mother and aunts to hallucinate that Pentheus himself is a bull. They chase him down and tear him apart. In this way, Dionysos demonstrates that he is, in fact, a powerful god.

The psychology of the puritanical Pentheus stands out. He main-tains an almost hysterical opposition to Dionysos. Pentheus stands for the manly virtues of a patriarchal culture. He controls a city that's pro-tected from the wider world within high walls. He values law and order.

By contrast, Dionysos and his follower are effeminate. His worship-pers are women. They wander in the wide-open fields. They eschew traditional Greek customs in favor of foreign ones. In short, Dionysos contradicts Pentheus' view of how the world should work. Pentheus knows nothing about what the Bacchae do in the fields, but his mind leaps to lewd behavior. In this way, Pentheus inadvertently divulges what lies in his own repressed subconscious. He starts to feel the trans-gressive impulses within himself. With just a thin pretext, that of scout-ing out the enemy, the follower easily persuades Pentheus to dress as a woman and become a Bacchant himself. Notice how Pentheus starts to enjoy dressing in drag:

DIONYSOS: You show the shape of one of Cadmus's daughters.
PENTHEUS: And I really seem to see two suns,
            And Thebes is doubled, even the seven-gated city;
            And you seem like a bull leading the way for us
            And to have sprouted horns with your strength.
            But are you sometimes an animal? For you have become a bull.
DIONYSOS: The god pursues his way with us under truce, though really he is
            Not well disposed. And now you see what is necessary for you to see.
PENTHEUS: So what do I look like? Hasn't this been Ino's posture
            And Agave's and my mother's?

(Bacchae 917–26)

Pentheus has succumbed to the psychosis of Dionysian worship. Zirin pointed out that seeing double is a common symptom of psychotic episodes. Pentheus seems detached from reality. He is wrapped up in his own petty concerns—he preens in his fawn skins and worries about his appearance—and does not respond directly to Dionysos or notice his ominous words. Pentheus exhibits further signs of dissociation in seeing Dionysos as a bull. Pentheus and the follower/Dionysos thus switch roles, with the disguised Pentheus now taking the effeminate part while Dionysos reveals his divine power by appearing as a bull, a symbol of virility. At the same time, Pentheus projects himself onto Dionysos, for he becomes the masculine bull that the Bacchic women tear apart. Pentheus offers a study of the power of unconscious impulses and how they can destroy us if we do not honor them but try to suppress them.

Zirin and I had such fascinating discussions that I wanted to dig deeper into *The Bacchae*. But Zirin did not recommend I read Dodds' *The Greeks and the Irrational*. Instead, he sent me to the library after quite a different work, *The Bacchants of Euripides and Other Essays* (1910) by a late Victorian critic, Arthur Verrall. Verrall had written an earlier book called *Euripides the Rationalist: A Study in the History of Art and Religion* (1895). Verrall saw Euripides as the enemy, not the exponent, of the irrational. And he has a point. Euripides questioned many traditional assumptions about humans and gods. In *Alcestis*, for example, Apollo granted Admetus, the king of Pherae, the favor of putting off the day he was fated to die if he could find someone to die in his place. Admetus' wife, Alcestis, agrees to take his place. The tragedy contrasts the rational courage and resolution of Alcestis with the irrational fear and cowardice of Admetus. According to Verrall, Euripides set up all the conflicts in his plays to demonstrate the triumph of rational thought over superstition.

Verrall argued the point programmatically. He returned to the theme again and again throughout his career. Verrall himself was a rationalist. No point can be valid unless proved by rational, scientific means. Euripides became his hero. The tragedian lived in a culture dominated by inherited belief in the gods and other supernatural forces, according to Verrall, and he used his gifts as a playwright to expose them as fraudulent. Although sometimes, for his own safety, Euripides had to conceal what he was trying to do under convoluted plots.

Verrall realized that *The Bacchae* posed the greatest challenge to his thesis:

> [I]n the *Bacchants*, and nowhere else among the tragedies of Euripides, we have a drama consisting, from first to last, of incidents which, upon the face of them and according to the prevalent belief of the persons represented, are miraculous and supernatural.[1]

If Verrall could crack this play, his thesis about Euripides would be unassailable. I imagine him taking his time to gather evidence and think through his argument. He hardly mentioned the play in *Euripides the Rationalist*, and he didn't analyze the play in a subsequent volume, either, *Essays on Four Plays of Euripides: Andromache, Helen, Heracles, Orestes* (1905). Verrall waited 15 years after his big book on Euripides till he made a frontal assault on *The Bacchae*.

Dodds and Zirin accepted the supernatural occurrences in the play as symbols of the human psyche. On principle, Verrall does not accept the supernatural as real in any sense because it has no rational basis. Since Euripides is a rationalist, Verrall reasons, he would not have accepted the supernatural as real, either. He would not have represented them in *The Bacchae* even for a dramatic conceit. Instead, he expects the discerning reader to see the miracles associated with Dionysos as mere frauds. Here, Verrall explains the episode where Pentheus tries to bind the follower/Dionysos but ends up wrestling with the bull:

> What [the follower/Dionysos] tells of his operations upon the mind of Pentheus [is] wild, impossible, destitute of confirmation, inconsistent with visible facts. The adept [follower] is able by suitable suggestion to excite, in those who passionately believe and habitually obey him, imaginative beliefs and even imaginary sensations, for which they themselves are prepared by confident expectancy. This agrees with nature, as we know it now and may presume it to have been known in the days of Euripides. But it does not follow that, by his mere will and pleasure, he could mislead and hallucinate a mind incredulous and hostile. Because the bacchants, at his suggestion, attribute his voice to Dionysus, and because one of them even sees a fire, it does not follow that Pentheus, without any preparation, would take a bull for a man; and the dramatist, by showing us the natural performance, gives us no reason to accept a report of the unnatural. And the facts, the words and behaviour of Pentheus, refute this as well as the rest. The hallucinations indeed, as such, Pentheus might be supposed to have forgotten; but his labours, his frantic efforts to extinguish the fire, his pursuit and assault of the phantom-prisoner—these, whether remembered or not, are *ex hypothesi* real, and their effect should be visible. The story leaves Pentheus "lying," as well he may, "exhausted." The words are scarcely said, when Pentheus himself comes out, vigorous as ever, so far as appears from the dialogue, both in body and mind![2]

A pagan god like Dionysos did not exist, thinks the Christian Verrall, and a critical intelligence such as Euripides wouldn't have believed anything so absurd. Therefore, the follower cannot be Dionysos in disguise; he must be a mountebank pretending to exercise divine powers in order to bring credulous people under his sway. Verrall knew about mesmerism, and he agrees that a strong personality can cause the mind of a willing subject to hallucinate. However, he cannot accept that a mesmerist could hypnotize as strong a character as Pentheus against his will. The follower of Dionysos merely claims to have done so in order to trick the Chorus.

For Verrall, Pentheus dies a martyr's death at the hands of the unreasoning horde of women. However, the play poses a challenge to this interpretation: If Pentheus aims to suppress a religion he knows is

fraudulent, why does he willingly put himself in the power of the follower of Dionysos? Why let the follower dress him up and lead him out
into the fields to slaughter? Verrall offers a rational answer:

> [W]e cannot suppose that the stranger, having got Pentheus to
> confer with him in the palace, makes an idiot of him by merely so
> willing, — how is it done, and how is the manner of it explained,
> as of course it must be, to the audience? Possibly that may not
> now be discoverable. The text of a dramatist, shorn of the action
> and not interpreted by directions, is but too likely to present, as
> the Greek tragedians do, some problems not determinable. But
> there are some indications, all pointing one way, which, so far as
> I know, have not been considered, and perhaps have not been
> noticed. Whether they are sufficient, it is for the reader to decide.
> I submit them for what they may be worth.
>
> Foremost, because most conspicuous, may be set the
> fact that, when Pentheus comes forth demented, the first
> symptom of his state is an affection not at all mystical, but
> bacchic in the most vulgar sense ... In plain terms ... the man
> is drunk. He sees double, like any toper reeling out of a wine-
> shop. Now surely it was a blunder in the dramatist, a mistake
> of judgement and taste, to put in this trait, unless he really
> means that the victim is intoxicated, and has taken something,
> some drink or drug, such as would naturally do the work.[3]

Verrall marks down to drunkenness the symptoms that Zirin perceived
as psychotic. Euripides could never have meant his rational hero to
abuse alcohol; Pentheus must have been drugged by the follower of
Dionysos. "The stranger comes from Asia Minor, a home of poisons
and poisoners," Verrall explains. "As an adept in ecstasies, a commu-
nicator of secret delights, he is not likely to be without experience
in drugs."[4] Thus, *The Bacchae* dramatizes a clash between the good
European Pentheus and an evil drug pusher from Asia who dupes him.

So we have diametrically opposed interpretations of the same play.
Verrall insists *The Bacchae* champions reason while Dodds argues that it
is an exploration of the irrational. These interpretations don't represent
solutions to a mere intellectual puzzle in which their authors invest little
personally. The work must have meant a great deal to its authors, for they
devoted a large portion of their lives to it. Verrall wrote three volumes
on Euripides in 15 years. Dodds wrote three books on the irrational over
three decades. Nor can the interpretations spring largely from the different
cultural and intellectual atmospheres in which the authors lived. Verrall

could have taken the irrational seriously if he wanted. The Romantics had created a vocabulary to describe the irrational, and their work remained current in late Victorian England. Moreover, many of Verrall's contemporary scholars wrote about Euripides, tragedy, myths, and religion with great understanding of the cultural norms of ancient Greece. In fact, he cites and tries to refute some of them in *The Bacchants of Euripides*. Dodds even drew on these sources for his own work. For his part, Dodds could have taken a more rationalist view of Euripides if he had wanted to. The power dynamics of *The Bacchae* easily lend themselves to a Marxist or feminist interpretation. Dodds chose to turn to the irrational instead.

These two English classicists, reading the same text, came to opposite conclusions because those interpretations must have satisfied different needs within each of them. Dodds was interested in depth. He wanted to penetrate the psychology driving extreme behavior. Verrall was interested in order. He wanted reassurance that a rational explanation underlies apparently irrational occurrences. Dodds and Verrall found meaning in two different ways of looking at the world. These aesthetic perspectives override other considerations. In fact, Verrall is still a source of amusement for classicists today. He illustrates the danger of making categorical assumptions and then bending the evidence preposterously to support them. The fact that Verrall pushes his arguments as far as he does shows the power of his compulsion for order. That is what fulfilled his soul's urge for meaning.

Meaning is aesthetic. It comes to us as a *feeling*. We like to think of the content as reasoned and defensible, but ultimately we adhere to a meaning because it satisfies us emotionally, regardless of how valid it is. We do not accept a logical argument because logic is epistemologically sound. Rather, we trust the argument because the form of logic feels right to us. Something motivates us to embrace it, maybe to act on it. Without the emotional tone that we attach to logic, the argument would make no impression on our minds. Verrall loved rationality. He loved it so much that he clung to it even when it led to what looks like nonsense to the rest of us. Other people don't trust logic. They find other things meaningful. Meanings that come from emotion, imagination, pleasure, or any other human faculty stimulate us in some way to pay attention to the world, apart from whether these impressions depict reality accurately.

The affinity we feel with certain emotional styles of meaning suggests they spring from deep within our unconscious. We read many books. We love the variety we find there. They make us think and feel many things. Nevertheless, our *experience* of these multiple meanings runs along just a few well-worn patterns. Eight archetypes or styles of meaning reflect the characteristic ways in which we encounter something significant.

The archetypes manifest themselves in simple storylines. Meaning occurs almost as a miniature drama where some action or setup prepares the way for a striking climax. Different setups and climaxes produce different experiences of meaning. The eight archetypes are as follows:

- Depth
- Revelation
- Recognition
- Boundary-crossing
- Novelty
- Beauty
- Order
- Tradition

Style 1: Depth. We experience depth as being drawn inward into an object, often in layers or by stations, where each successive layer feels more significant than the last. Recall C.G. Jung's dream about the house in which the farther he descended, the further back in archeological time he went. At every step downward, he confronted a more alien culture, and therefore, every descending level evoked more wonder. In *The Doors of Perception*, Aldous Huxley talks about the experience of depth conveyed by garments in Flemish Renaissance paintings. The deep folds stand out because of the sharp contrast of light and shade between the peaks and valleys of the fabric, the richness of the brocades, and their jewel tones. The image draws us in and makes us feel we have entered a world of greater intensity, whose significance transcends the object depicted. He likens the experience to the hallucinations caused by psychotropic drugs.

In literature, the simplest lines often imply tremendous things such as the first line from the gospel of *John* [1:1]: "In the beginning was the Word, and the Word was with God, and the Word was God."[5] We could spend a lifetime following out all the ramifications. "In the beginning" suggests that the essence of the universe appears at its starting point. Probably the author means the starting point in time—the creation—but we could just as easily interpret it as a philosophical starting point, the universe's fundamental principle. "[T]he word was with God" indicates that word and God are distinct although, for that moment "in the beginning," they coincided. God knew the word at that point and may still do, but potentially it has abandoned him so that he does not know it now. "The Word was God" states an identity a bit at odds with the preceding clause yet still in the past tense. We can look at it from two perspectives. On one hand, the clause could mean that the distinct being God addressed us through language, including but not limited to the scriptures. We can understand what he wants by reading or hearing it. On the other hand, the word itself could be God. We do not have to peer through the text dimly into heaven to see him; we see God directly when we look at the text. Of course, "In the beginning" alludes to the first verses of *Genesis*, where the creation occurs through a speech act: "And God said, 'Let there be light'; and there was light [*Genesis* 1:3]."[6] Perhaps we exercise divine creative power when we ourselves speak. Each of these interpretations implies an entire theology. The simplicity and openness of John's language invites us to read vastly more into it than appears on the surface.

Style 2: Revelation. We experience revelation as the answer to a question that requires hard work to solve. We love the climactic scene of a murder mystery in which all the characters gather together to hear the detective explain the case step by step and then reveal the identity of the killer. The hidden becomes known, and this paradigm strikes us as more meaningful than if we knew the secret all along. In the Eleusinian Mysteries, the priests of Demeter would show initiates the cult objects sacred to the goddess only at the end of ten days of ceremonies and processions. Afterward, the initiates would have to keep the secret from noninitiates or face execution. The elaborate religious drama, with its final unveiling, emphasizes the importance of its content. In *The Origin of Species*, Charles Darwin unveiled the idea of evolution by natural selection, which drives the similarity and diversity of life forms on earth. The idea strikes us as powerful in part because of the complicated scientific analysis required to demonstrate the workings of evolution beneath the static appearance of species that we can observe in the world.

Style 3: Recognition. We experience recognition when we discover something about ourselves or others that we knew all along but didn't acknowledge. Many self-help books aim to show readers how to fulfill themselves. Sophocles' tragedy *Oedipus Rex* starts with Thebes suffering from a plague that kills many people. In an oracle, Apollo declares that he sent the plague to punish the city for harboring a person guilty of murdering the former king. Oedipus, the city's dictator, vows to find and punish the guilty party. He conducts a high-handed investigation, accusing even his closest associates of being the criminal. At the end of the play, Oedipus discovers that he himself is the guilty party. He had unwittingly killed his biological father, the former king, in a road rage incident and married his biological mother just as a prophecy foretold before his birth. The prophecy had frightened Oedipus' parents. They gave the baby to a shepherd to expose on a hillside, but the shepherd took pity on Oedipus and raised him as his own son. Others know or suspect the truth. They taunt Oedipus with his shady origin. His mother, now wife, begs him to drop the case. Oedipus plunges ahead anyway. We're not sure whether it's because he can't imagine himself guilty or because he feels the adopted child's urge to know where he comes from. In any case, the truth comes as such a shock that Oedipus can't bear it—he pokes his own eyes out with a pin.

On the road to Emmaus, the risen Jesus appears to the disciples, who don't recognize him at first:

> That very day two [disciples] were going to a village named Emma'us, about seven miles from Jerusalem, and talking with each other about all these things that had happened. While they were talking and discussing together, Jesus himself drew near and went with them. But their eyes were kept from recognizing him …
>
> So they drew near to the village to which they were going. He appeared to be going further, but they constrained him, saying, "Stay with us, for it is toward evening and the day is now far spent." So he went to stay with them. When he was at the table with them, he took the bread and blessed, and gave it to them. And their eyes were opened and they recognized him; and he vanished out of their sight.
>
> [*Luke* 24:13–31][7]

The disciples had heard Jesus preach about the resurrection—indeed, they were discussing it when he met them on the road. But there is a difference between taking in the idea intellectually and confronting it in the flesh. In the Emmaus story, the apostles recognize Jesus in the figure of a stranger. They realize that they must treat others as Jesus, must honor the divine in everyone. The unique Jesus they had contemplated previously vanishes, and they are free to offer hospitality to others they might meet in this way.

Style 4: Boundary-crossing. We experience boundary-crossing when someone pushes through an assumed limit into an area with different rules. Stories of innovation often convey this kind of meaning. In 1965, Dick Fosbury invented the technique of leaping backward over the bar in the high jump. Up to that point, high jumpers used the front roll, approaching the bar on a slant, leaping from one foot, kicking the other leg up, and rolling the chest over the bar. Fosbury would twist as he leapt so that his back would face the bar while his body elevated. He'd arch his back as it cleared and then raise his legs straight as he descended so as not to hit the bar. He won the gold medal in the 1968 Olympics in Mexico City. Since then, high jumpers cannot be competitive unless they use the Fosbury Flop.

Apple Computer popularized the graphical user interface in its first personal computers. Previously, computers had text-based interfaces. The computer displayed all information in text, and users had to type out the right sequence of characters in a command line in order to get a computer to do anything. Users had to memorize the correct syntax for each command—boot up a diskette, generate a list of files, open a file, make edits, and so on. The graphical user interface displayed information about the computer pictorially. Thus, people could use a mouse to perform basic functions, such as double clicking on the image of a file or folder to open it. Even novices could quickly navigate around a computer and become productive. The graphical user interface made computers accessible to everyone, not just the technically adept. No company would offer a mass-market device today unless it had one.

Igor Stravinsky introduced modernism to Western music in 1913 with his score for the ballet *The Rite of Spring*. All the greats, from Bach to Brahmns, used a seven-tone scale. Audiences expected it. Stravinsky used an atonal technique in which the urgent, driving sounds mimicked the action of the dancers. At the first performance in Paris, *The Rite of Spring* shocked the audience so much it rioted. After Stravinsky, classical composers can't make it into the top rank simply by writing beautiful or passionate music; they must challenge audiences and be technically innovative as well.

Style 5: Novelty. We experience novelty as the sudden appearance of something we never imagined existing or being possible. Novelty gives us a glimpse into a realm of new possibilities. Realistic depiction of humans had dominated Western art since the fourteenth century. Faces might be caricatured or stylized, yet they remained three-dimensional and recognizable as individuals. In 1907, Pablo Picasso painted a study of five naked prostitutes in the style of Cezanne, with the bodies and three of the faces simplified into geometric shapes. Picasso had seen tribal masks from Africa in Paris museums. That inspired him to paint the other two faces in his group portrait as masks, their features generic, flattened on the picture plane, and represented with distorted perspective. Picasso had broken painting's tether to realism in order to find whole new dimensions of his subjects' character to represent. The two masked figures represent not individuals or even types but primal energies that they channel in their profession. *Les Demoiselles D'Avignon* was the first modernist painting. Under its influence, Western art exploded with experimentation and abstraction that continue today.

Novelty does not have to come from geniuses like Picasso, who rapidly developed several different forms of abstract painting. People may not realize the novelty of what they have done and, therefore, may never exploit it themselves. The ancient Greek general and historian Xenophon stumbled upon the invention of the novel. From the beginning in Greece, narratives took the form of myths and legends. Herodotus and Thucydides invented narrative history to give an accurate picture of recent events. Xenophon was a mercenary soldier from Athens who led a battalion of Greeks to fight for Cyrus the Younger in 401 B.C. Cyrus sought to overthrow his older brother, who was then the emperor of Persia. The rebellion failed, and Xenophon led his troops on a perilous march back to Greece, where he wrote an account called the *Anabasis* or *Retreat*. Xenophon also wrote a continuation of the history of the Peloponnesian war, which had stopped at 411 B.C. because of Thucydides' death. Xenophon wrote a book about the Spartan constitution. He wrote philosophical dialogues featuring Socrates. He fused many of these genres together in the *Cyropaedia* or *The Education of Cyrus* (370 B.C.). The *Cyropaedia* ostensibly recounts the history of Cyrus the Great, the sixth-century founder of the Persian Empire, especially his education and political struggles before attaining power. However, the book includes legends about Cyrus and blends in a description of the characteristics and political philosophy of Cyrus the Younger, for whom Xenophon fought. Thus, the book synthesizes the portrait of a character who never existed yet relates his story as though it had actually happened. Xenophon did not realize he had invented a new form of narrative. He didn't follow it up with other books that developed the genre. But some ancient authors wrote novels such as *The Alexander Romance*, about Alexander the Great, which portray their subjects in similar ways. Xenophon's *Cyropaedia* also influenced early modern novels such as Philip Sidney's *Arcadia*.

Style 6: Beauty. We experience beauty as the arrangement of parts into definite forms. Only a craven person could resist the sweetness of the slow movement of Beethoven's ninth symphony or the soul and energy of van Gogh at his best. Or consider Ezra Pound's *Canto* III, which starts with the poet in Venice and jumps to other images:

> I sat on the Dogana's steps
> For the gondolas cost too much, that year,
> And there were not "those girls," there was one face,
> And the Buccentoro twenty yards off, howling "Stretti,"
> And the lit-cross beams, that year, in the Morosini,
> And peacocks in Koré's house, or there may have been.
>   Gods float in the azure air,
> Bright gods and Tuscan, back before dew was shed.
> Light: and the first light, before ever dew was fallen ...[8]

Forget what this passage is trying to say. Ignore the many allusions in it. Let the sensuality of the individual pieces wash over you. Like an ancient epic poem, it features the stringing together of phrases through the liberal use of "and." Everything connects to everything else. It reaches simple, Biblical grandeur ("Light: and the first light ..."). The passage contains incredibly rich imagery, expressed through concrete word choices ("lit-cross beams," "peacocks in Koré's house") and exotic vocabulary ("Buccentoro," "Morosini"). The world appears both accessible ("I sat on the Dogana's steps") and divine ("Gods float in the azure air"). The passage offers so many riches that we sit in the midst of it, like Pound on the Dogana's steps, our head in a pleasant whirl trying to take it all in. The apparently disparate images and ideas come together into an emergent form that we feel rather than understand. The poem's very beauty is the meaning: this is the way the world is supposed to be; it is supposed to be enchanting, achingly beautiful. The world is like this innately if we know how to see.

Style 7: Order. We experience order as the logical connection between parts to form a larger, coherent system. The science of geology as practiced today started with the publication in 1830 of Charles Lyell's *Principles of Geology.* Before then, geology consisted of isolated observations (e.g., the presence of fossils in mountains), unsubstantiated theories (landforms were created by volcanic activity), and little access to what lies beneath the earth's surface. This state of knowledge left many questions: Are fossils found in mountains because the earth generates animals and plants spontaneously? Why is coal found in some places in the earth but not others? Lyell proposed a comprehensive set of geologic processes to explain rock formations. For instance, volcanic activity thrusts magma to the surface, which hardens into rocks, and wind and water erode these rocks, which settle into sedimentary layers. By systemizing geology, Lyell enabled scientists to explore the earth by proposing hypotheses and doing field work or experiments to test them. For example, coal is carbonized trees found only in certain layers of rock laid down during a geological epoch when vast forests covered the earth. Geologists can test this theory by determining which rock layers coal deposits appear in. Judging by how slowly the geologic processes we can observe unfold, Lyell showed that the earth had existed in an exponentially longer timescale than humans had imagined up to this point—millions of years rather than thousands. This framework furnished a critical piece for scientists who came after him, especially Darwin. Evolutionary processes also unfold with imperceivable slowness and, therefore, become possible only with a geologic timescale.

Adam Smith's *The Wealth of Nations* launched the discipline of economics by sketching the laws underlying hitherto puzzling economic phenomena such as international trade or price movements. Up to that point, people observed economic phenomena (e.g., gold draining out of a country) but had no way to analyze why they occurred. Or people proposed systems without any basis in fact. Francois Quesnay proposed that farms would become 10% more productive each year indefinitely if the farmer were unburdened with taxes and could reinvest his profits in the land. Smith showed that the returns from the farmer's investments would eventually taper off (the law of diminishing returns). Thus, Smith started a systematic investigation that economists have built upon ever since.

Style 8: Tradition. We experience tradition as a sense of continuity over time. Theocritus inaugurated the pastoral tradition in poetry in the third century B.C. with idylls about the simple lives of shepherds, filled with love affairs and singing contests, as a contrast to the sophisticated urban life he and his fellow poets and readers led in the Hellenistic Mediterranean. Theocritus inspired Vergil, who also wrote about shepherds although he turned his *Eclogues* into commentaries about contemporary Roman life and politics. Dante revived the pastoral genre at the very end of his life by writing two Vergilian eclogues but made them into allegories with obscure allusions. Boccaccio and Petrarch followed Dante's lead by writing pastoral verse, in part as satires on modern life, in part as elegies to dead friends and lost simplicity. Giovanni Baptista Spagnuoli developed the genre further by composing eclogues to attack the abuses of the church and to give advice to young people. Spagnuoli's eclogues gave Shakespeare material for his festive comedies, such as *As You Like It*, which compare the structured, corrupt life of the court with the freedom and poverty of the country. And so on.

Thus, we understand one work by looking at the work of predecessors which inspired it. In retrospect, we label this chain of influence a "tradition," which those within it grasped with varying degrees of awareness. In a tradition, each person adds something to the legacy of the past. Or we may describe a sequence of writers, works, or actions that have loose connections to one another. These recent titles, *The American Tradition in Literature*, *The American Political Tradition*, *The American Intellectual Tradition*, and *The American Military Tradition*, apply the frame of tradition in retrospect to describe common, often unconscious characteristics that extend across time.

The eight archetypes of meaning describe emotional contours although we have been trained to look past them and to see only the idea at the center, not the feelings that surround it. We value the pearl for the sand grain instead of the layers of nacre coating it. From the time we start reading in school, we learn to think of meaning as existing within the text. We employ various interpretive methods to bring the meaning out. The text remains the object of inquiry.

Such critical investigations of the text disrespect the reader. We insist that reading is important, that it matters in the world. However, the only way it can be important is through the reader; it must affect the reader's life fundamentally. If we expect serious readers to hang their lives on a book, the drama must occur inside them, not on the page. Some mechanism of the soul converts the words into thoughts that readers believe enough to test on themselves, often at some risk. None of these things happens unless readers put emotional force behind them. We need a language to articulate the various transformations that occur within readers, one that doesn't attribute everything to the text. The examples above that illustrate the eight archetypes point to the fulfillment of readers' common emotional needs. Sometimes, we need a revelation to turn a gray world into exciting colors. Or we look for order when the world threatens chaos. Or we thirst for beauty and so on. In this way, the eight archetypes of meaning help us to explore readers' experiences without plunging back into the text.

The archetypes start to demarcate the large, hitherto empty region between the extremes where we conventionally allow the text to function for readers. On one hand, we make the humanistic assumption that the text appeals to readers universally. "I am a human," said the Roman playwright Terence. "Nothing human is foreign to me." The New Critics in the middle of the twentieth century believed each text contained a single line of meaning that the author expected every reader to follow. People would inevitably grasp this meaning if they read acutely enough. On the other hand, we acknowledge that readers can relate to books subjectively. A particular reader has lived in a way that other readers have not, and he or she relates the text to that experience. Life as a woman or an African-American permits us to see meanings in a text that escape people with other social profiles. Or we accept as legitimate any interpretation of a poem simply because someone read it that way.

The archetypes of meaning strike a compromise between the universal and the subjective. We have all encountered depth, recognition, innovation, and the other patterns. We know what they feel like. Nevertheless, we each differ in the emphasis we give to them. We need different types of meaning at different times, depending on our circumstances. And our character tends to favor one or a few archetypes over others just as depth mattered most to Dodds and order to Verrall. Unconsciously, we search for meaning in a text based on our predilections.

The meaning of a text arises from the interaction of the words with the needs that the reader brings to them. The eight archetypes give us a way to distinguish between the various demands a reader might make. We do not have to see any single interpretation as unavoidable. Instead, we can view it as a choice determined by the inner necessity of the reader. Again, we *experience* meaning rather than deduce it or absorb it from somewhere else, and that experience comes in the form of a feeling. We can, therefore, ascribe to ourselves—to our own perceptions, our own creativity—a significance that we had before projected onto the text or the author. In effect, the archetypes convert what previously seemed to be solid literary structures into suppositions that must prove their utility to us.

For example, some readers talk about tradition as though it were an objective reality. They will describe, say, the "Western literary tradition," by tracing themes, such as individualism and realism, across centuries. These themes supposedly explain who we are today and why we think the way we do. In this way, tradition tells a coherent story about a past that actually consisted of many different kinds of books, written by many different kinds of authors, in many different kinds of circumstances, for many different purposes, at many different times, in many different places. Nothing obligates us to see threads of continuity in these works, but readers choose to impose the framework of tradition on authors and texts because it satisfies their need to have a precedent. It legitimizes today's ideas.

Any form of meaning, including tradition, does violence to its subject because we cannot help seeing the subject through the filter of our own needs. The invention of a tradition requires readers to pick out a specific set of texts, between which they trace lines of influence that tell a coherent story, and to ignore other texts that don't fit the narrative. "Western literature" starts with Homer and continues with the great books up to James Joyce's *Ulysses* and beyond. Along the way, we omit or ignore hundreds of "lesser" writers—Statius and Samuel Daniel and many more authors once important but now scarcely known. Nevertheless, we would be able to choose another set of texts from the whole universe of Western books and thereby construct quite a different Western tradition. In fact, we could create many different Western literary traditions, depending on the books we select. Each tradition would highlight some authors and ideas at the expense of other authors and ideas. Imagine Shakespeare falling out of our collective memory—it wouldn't be the first time that had happened. By proposing one particular tradition, we don't "discover" some objective reality about Western literature that always awaited us on library shelves. Rather, we trick ourselves into making the creative leap of inventing a Western tradition. We wish the comfortable feeling of tradition were real, so we treat it as such.

The emotional allure of any type of meaning captivates us. Once we find a satisfactory interpretation of something we hold it so close that we narrow our field of view and don't bother to look for other possibilities. If we make the eight archetypes explicit, we can use them to question our own emotional needs and perhaps gain a little more freedom of thought.

If we trace meanings back to the eight archetypes, we can follow out at least seven other routes that will lead us to new meanings beside the one that we are most drawn to. I happened to pick the archetype of depth for my reading of *The Bacchae*. I didn't have to. I have had experiences of meaning that fit into each of the eight categories. All eight are emotionally accessible to me. If I see meaning as my own feeling, not something inherent in the text, I gain the freedom to choose the emotional framework within which to read it. What would *The Bacchae* mean from the point of view of beauty or boundary-crossing? I can play with the archetypes until I find the emotional range that most satisfies the needs of the moment.

Awareness of the emotional underpinning of meaning gives us more control over the feelings we experience when we read so that we can turn in many directions until we earn the biggest profit from the book. If we focus on what we feel, we no longer have to be the recipients or excavators of an external meaning. We can take control of meaning by deciding for ourselves what it will look like. Think of the surprise and pleasure that rush through us when we discover something. It's different from the surprise and pleasure when we encounter beauty. Although meaning can evoke various feelings, the patterns of meaning fulfill the same general function and are interchangeable in that way. We can try them out one by one, applying them to an object that interests us until we find the pattern that suits us best. Once we know the pattern, we can fill in the content of the meaning by rearranging our thoughts about the object. I'll provide an extended example of how to do this in a later chapter.

NOTES

1 Arthur Verrall, *The Bacchants of Euripides and Other Essays* (Cambridge: Cambridge University Press, 1910), pp. 1–2.
2 Ibid., pp. 73–74.

3 Ibid., pp. 107–8.
4 Ibid., p. 109.
5 *The New Oxford Annotated Bible with the Apocrypha*, eds., Herbert G. May and Bruce M. Metzger (New York: Oxford University Press, 1977) p. 1286.
6 Ibid., p. 1.
7 Ibid., pp. 1283–4.
8 Ezra Pound, *The Cantos of Ezra Pound* (New York: New Directions Books, 1971), p. 11.

PART II

Ways of reading

CHAPTER 6

Intimacy with books

Every form of reading implies a mode of being in the world. Every theory of reading assumes something about human nature. Any way of reading is valuable not for what it reveals about books but to the extent that it connects us to the world.

Familiar ways of reading can inadvertently limit us. Most readers know Samuel Taylor Coleridge's statement that reading works of imagination requires a "willing suspension of disbelief." More fully, Coleridge wanted the characters in his poems "to transfer from our inward nature a human interest and a semblance of truth sufficient to procure for these shadows of imagination that willing suspension of disbelief for the moment, which constitutes poetic faith."[1]

This formulation presumes that some detached intelligence resides within the reader and passes judgment on everything that unrolls before his eyes. This aloof faculty of "disbelief" echoes John Locke's image of the mind as a wax tablet, passively absorbing the Newtonian particles bombarding it from a universe of sterile matter. Humans cannot know the world directly but only through the mediation of sense impressions. Individual corpuscles of light enter the eye. Our mind assembles them into an image. We identify the image by reference to memories of past experience—does this latest image look like anything we have seen before? Then we must question whether we can believe what our senses seem to tell us. Is that an actual tree or merely a picture of a tree? At best, the image bears "a semblance of truth." We continually ask ourselves "Is this real or not?" as we go through life, and our physiology constrains us to engage with the world through acts of interpretation. Thus, we start with an innate bias toward skepticism, according to Coleridge.

We must turn off this critical faculty temporarily in order to enjoy literature. Literature creates images in our mind that recall our own experiences or that suggest experiences which could be real though we know they are not. In order to feel them as true, we must override the disbelief that is inherent to our human nature. Accordingly, Coleridge wants to supplement this skeptical self with a second self, no less diffident, that generates feelings. This faculty creates sympathies with the thoughts and situations of the characters we read about. We might explain the sympathetic faculty today as mirror neurons, which allow us to observe other people's reactions to events and to put ourselves in their place mentally. From the sensations that impress the images of other people on our minds, we reconstitute within ourselves the same feelings they are experiencing. We do not have to react mechanically to external stimuli like an automaton, Coleridge asserts. Instead, we can also feel and respond with feeling.

For Coleridge, reading mediates between isolated hearts the way an aged nurse in an old play conveys notes between two lovers forbidden to meet. We communicate with others through the medium of printed words yet remain locked in the apartness of our individual minds. A well-written poem allows us to feel what other people at a distance feel. At any moment, though, Coleridge fears, the critical faculty can reassert itself to sever even these sympathies. Disbelief threatens the reader constantly because the feelings conveyed by the text are secondary creations and not fundamental particles of the universe such as the photons striking our retina. Hence the pattern of Romantic tragedy in which materialistic considerations drive a wedge between two warm hearts drawn to each other in this cold world.

We still share Coleridge's understanding about how we relate to the world. We point to studies that have found reading literature increases our empathy for others. We live separated from our fellow humans in this world, and literature makes a virtual connection. We read to understand what it's like for different nations, classes, political persuasions, races, ethnicities, religions, genders, sexual orientations—all of the divides that baffle us. Literature enables us to see across them.

However, we don't really experience reading as just a medium of communication between separated minds. Reading feels more intimate than that. I chose to write a paper on Fyodor Dostoevsky's *The Idiot* for my first college English class. Somewhere in the middle of reading the novel's 500 or 600 pages, I made a mental note of a passage involving a minor character that struck me as interesting. Some days later, when I had finished the book, I decided to write my term paper about that passage. I had a vivid impression of where it occurred in my volume. It lay in the middle of the book on a recto page about two thirds of the way down. I knew what the page looked like—I could picture the paragraph blocks in my mind. I flipped back and found the page and the passage within seconds.

I do not have a photographic memory. I'm not good at facial recognition, either, but I can pick my wife out of a crowd because I know her in a way that only love allows. My heart is always looking for her. Similarly, I could find the passage in *The Idiot* so quickly because I had a deep emotional connection with the text. It appealed to me with a kind of intimacy such as we share with a lover. We see the object of our desire, and something immediately turns us on. Our faculties become more acute. We drink in every delicious detail. When we read, the words become animate. We grasp them instantly. They strike our mind as a single, recognizable image, not as an assemblage of letters that we must first synthesize into a word and then define according to some dictionary we carry in our head. The mechanical decipherment implied by Locke's corpuscles and wax tablets doesn't describe what happens when we read. Rather, sentences unroll fluidly in our mind in perfect comprehension, one after another. The prose style and narrative carry us forward with momentum. We enter a flow state. We savor every nuance of what happens on the page. The text acquires multiple dimensions. We see the logic of the argument, the rhetorical devices, the rhythm of the sentences, the ambiguities and multiple meanings, the emotional import, and so on. As a result, we develop intimacy with the book. Our mind floats above the linguistic matrix, entwined with the text like embracing lovers hovering over the landscape in a Chagall painting.

We fall in love with the images that books project of themselves. How many times have you found that a glance at the cover of a random book induced you to pick it up and read only to discover that you actually liked it? You *can* judge a book by its cover. How many times have you heard someone say a couple of off-handed sentences about a book and felt an urge to read it immediately?

Every book is an object imbued with feelings. It exercises some unique attraction or repulsion on us. The force of this attraction resides in the specific artifact. I do not own Joseph Conrad's *Under Western Eyes*. I own a Doubleday Anchor edition that retailed for $1.45 when it published in 1963, a mass-market paperback with a worn blue cover and four or five parallel cracks running down its spine. The cover has photos of the Winter Palace in St. Petersburgh, Russia, and of Geneva, Switzerland. The book has a specific type face and a specific smell. I wouldn't necessarily like *Under Western Eyes* as well if I owned a different edition. For 35 years, I have owned a Signet Classic edition of Hamlin Garland's *Main Traveled Roads*, a book of short stories set in the northern prairie of the late nineteenth century. I like Signet Classic editions generally, and the text on the back cover makes *Main Traveled Roads* sound interesting. I do want to read it. I tried a few times. But I couldn't even force myself to do it. My copy, the size of a mass-market paperback, has a hardcover school binding. The sterility of its machine-smooth white boards and squared spine and corners puts me off. One day, I will go to the library and look for a different edition of *Main Traveled Roads*, something warmer and more comfortable. I will take it to a cozy chair for quiet enjoyment.

Books project an image beyond the literal features of their design. At a bookstore, I once found a used copy of Flaubert's *Trois Contes* (*Three Tales*), published by Garnier-Flammarion. I bought it for $3.75 with the aspiration that some day I would brush up my French enough to read it with appreciation. There for 15 years the thin mass-market paperback sat shyly on a bookshelf. (I love mass-market paperbacks because they fit in one hand comfortably like a vacation thriller.) I carted it with me through many moves. Occasionally, I would encounter the volume when I was packing books in a moving carton or rearranging my shelves. One night, the soul of the book summoned me in a dream just as Hermes exhorted the sleeping Agamemnon in the *Iliad*. I saw the name **FLAMMARION** appear before my eyes, standing out on the cover in thick, crimson capitals. The letters cut sharply although rounded corners softened the stark lines a little. The boldness of the type made a nice contrast with the thin black lines and delicate coloring of the woodcut of St. Julian the Hospitaler on the cover.

When I awoke the next morning, I went to my bookshelf and pulled out *Trois Contes* from behind a pile of contemporary novels. The heavy plastic-coated cover bowed slightly. Scuffs and marks offered evidence of its previous owner. Only the light shades of the woodcut relieved the black and white of the rest of the volume. "GF FLAMMARION GF FLAMMARION GF FLAMMARION" in black hollow type was repeated discreetly around the perimeter of the cover. But the glowing red **FLAMMARION** such as I saw pop out in my dream appeared nowhere on the book, evidence of its divine origin.

I opened the book and read the first two sentences of "Un Coeur Simple," the first tale:

> Pendant un demi-siècle, les bourgeoises de Pont-l'Évêque
> envièrent à Mme Aubain sa servent Félicité.

Pour cent francs par an, elle faisait la cuisine et le ménage, cousait, lavait, repassait, savait brider un cheval, engraisser les volailles, batter le beure, et resta fidèle à sa maîtresse,— qui cependant n'était pas une personne agréable.[2]

The large, comfortable type enticed me. I did not know all the vocabulary. I thought "engraisser les volailles" might mean "grease the window sashes." I looked up the words in my French-English dictionary and found they meant "fatten the hens." I decided it was time to work my way through the book. And I did, sometimes looking up each word in my dictionary, but persevering because of the pleasure of reading that volume. The image of the book, my desire for it, sustained me through what might otherwise have been a tedious, torturous task.

The images of books are multifaceted, most often consisting of hints and intimations, like obscure openings of a cave that lead down to deep, expansive caverns. You have to follow your intuition to find them. When I was writing my thesis about the prosody of modern verse in school, the project took longer than I care to remember. After a good amount of reading over several years, I still hadn't got to the point where I saw what I needed to write. My attention wandered. I wanted to read something different from what I had been reading for my research. Reason told me to resist the temptation to escape from the task at hand, but I gave into it anyway. Henry James' *The Golden Bowl* suddenly looked irresistible to me. *The Golden Bowl* is an example of the author's mature style, in which James packs convoluted sentences into long, dense paragraphs. This sample describes how the main character, Maggie Verver, strives to maintain her position in upper-middle-class English society:

> She knew accordingly nothing but harmony, she diffused restlessly nothing but peace—an extravagant expressive aggressive peace, not incongruous after all with the solid calm of the place; a kind of helmeted trident-shaking *pax Britannica*.
>
> The peace, it must be added, had become, as the days elapsed, a peace quite generally animated and peopled— thanks to that fact of the presence of "company" in which Maggie's ability to preserve an appearance had learned from so far back to find its best resource. It wasn't inconspicuous, it was in fact striking, that this resource just now seemed to meet in the highest degree every one's need: quite as if every one were, by the multiplication of human objects in the scene, by the creation, by the confusion of fictive issues, hopeful of escaping somebody else's notice.[3]

Normally prose sentences average about 20 words; these three of James average 45 words. They make few concrete references, nor do they unfold smoothly. Instead, James keeps inserting phrases that qualify the main idea and leave you hanging for a while before he brings you around to finish the point. These sentences also include colloquial phrases and shifts of direction such as we make in conversation or in our own thoughts. James' prose takes concentration to follow and not lose the thread of the narrative. If you give it that extra attention, though, his prose slows the mind right down into a hypnotically satisfying rhythm. Read James in long stretches, and you realize that his unusual style well captures the subtle inflections of people's stream of consciousness as they constantly adjust to the people around them. I am thinking my thoughts. I then see you thinking your thoughts, and that awareness alters the flow of my thoughts.

Actually, this is exactly the idea I needed for my thesis. For modern poets likewise strive to express the rhythm of thought in the apparently irregular patterns of their verse. Giving into my irrational urge for Henry James led me to what I needed for an unrelated task. I might have continued with my systematic research and never found this insight and never reached the point where I could write my thesis. But I did reach it now and finished the task in a few months. In this way, the reader's soul calls for particular food, and the image of a book lures the soul that needs to feed on it.

Reading as an engagement with the image of a book creates a more direct connection than a "suspension of disbelief." The meaning happens as an immediate experience rather than through the decipherment of stimuli and communications. We give ourselves to the text, which decides where we will go and what we will find next. At any moment, the book may disclose ravishing beauty or annihilate our self-regard. Still, we read on, absorbing whatever we discover like a traveler walking through a strange landscape. Caught up in the moment, we do not distinguish between it and ourselves. We are bound together as one. The book becomes our soul—too important for us to turn away, no matter what fearful shade ascends from the deeper underworld to confront us.

John Keats expressed this idea in a letter he wrote to his brothers the same year (1817) that Coleridge published his famous formula about reading:

> [I]t struck me what qualities went to form a Man of Achievement, especially in Literature, and which Shakespeare possessed so enormously—I mean *Negative Capability*, that

is, when a man is capable of being in uncertainties, mysteries, doubts, without any irritable reaching after fact and reason …[4]

Negative capability proposes a more radical philosophy than temporarily suspending disbelief in fictitious sensations. It involves the eclipse of the ego, whose function is to organize perceptions around itself in order to make sense of them. Keats asks us to let go of ourselves—of Coleridge's standoffish self, which watches and feels but cannot engage with the world directly—so that we can immerse ourselves in the world, not rationalize it away. If we have negative capability, phenomena strike us without being interpreted first. They retain their primordial energy.

Keats totters toward a language to help us engage intelligently with the unknown. "Uncertainties, mysteries, doubts" describe our experience of it (while "fact and reason" provide currency for the known). All three terms reveal an innate human capability to perceive the unknown anywhere, to sense that dimension in any encounter, however familiar. Think of the people we know most intimately. We know their likes and dislikes. We know their personalities. Our relationships enjoy stable bonds. We can predict how they will react in any situation. We render them elaborately in our hearts and imagination so that we feel we know all about them. But they still do things so unexpected, often at moments of crisis, that we wonder whether we ever really knew them. The unaccountable opinion, the strange hesitation when we assumed a wholehearted response, the next step that seems logical and inevitable yet is balked at reveal the vast uncertainty beneath the verisimilitude of our mental model of them.

Think of activities you have performed dozens, maybe hundreds of times—a route you have driven, a food you have eaten, a task you do at work. You do it by rote. One day, you stop in the middle of the routine as though snapping out of a reverie. You don't know where you are; you don't know how to get where you want to go. You don't know whether you love that dish or hate it. You wonder if anyone at work would notice if you omitted that task. One minute you are certain; the next you are disoriented. Where did that doubt come from? The possibility lurked there all along. Consciousness is a veneer.

Uncertainties, mysteries, and doubts crack open the known world for us. We glimpse the darkness through the fissures in a façade that had seemed so definite—perhaps oppressively so. We could slip through any one of these openings into the indeterminate realm of the unknown. We could satisfy our curiosity or face our fear, and from there, we could continue on into the darkness, moving from experience to experience, discovery to discovery.

Someone with negative capability experiences a text the same as any concrete phenomenon in the world. When we read, uncertainties, mysteries, and doubts break the text's shining surface of inevitability. Our facility with language allows us to skate from sentence to sentence, which glide by in perfect clarity while we're reading them. Then, something forces us to pause and consider whether we truly understand what the words mean. A friend of mine reinterpreted the narrative tone of Gabriel García Márquez's *One Hundred Years of Solitude* based on three words spoken in response to a massacre of peasants by soldiers. García Márquez's English translator had rendered *el puto mundo* as a detached pronouncement, "the whorish world," whereas an angry "the fucking world" better renders the sense in vernacular Spanish.[5]

A philosophy professor once asked me to translate a key passage for a paper he was writing about Thomas Aquinas' theory of free will. He had read the passage himself but wasn't satisfied he understood it properly. I worked from a photocopy, so I don't even know which work this comes from. The Latin text reads just as awkwardly as my translation:

> ... as happens when someone acts out of custom or habit or unconsciously. Whoever follows his own custom for good or ill does not really consider how something favorable is chosen by it, nor does he ever by any chance attempt to employ that habit; but by a certain comparison he rejects and accepts that thing, yet if he had brought them together, as long as he thus accepts that opposite thing to which he turns, it follows that it is chosen really by a certain comparison. One free action is to choose our innate and first movements by comparison.

This was the only translation that made grammatical sense to me. I showed it to my friend and said, "I don't see how it can mean anything else." He agreed—my version matched his own understanding. Still, neither of us felt confident we had extracted all the possibilities. The very awkwardness of the text suggested that we had not settled on the indisputable meaning. Others remained possible even if we couldn't see them at the moment. As a result, a large residue of doubt remained from our transaction with Aquinas' text. It waits in the back of our mind for a new thought to occur or for us to read or learn something that throws new light on the passage.

The longer we allow the imagination to work on something, the greater the chance new ideas and experiences will emerge. But the work comes at the psychic cost of insecurity. We feel impatient amid uncertainties, mysteries, and doubt. They irk us. Fear stirs inside. We sense the beginnings of confusion and disorientation. We don't want to go so far into the maze that we can't find our way back out. We might lose the certainties upon which we founded our life and identity. Some of us have a high tolerance for ambiguity, some of us low. Regardless, at a certain point, we each reach for "fact and reason" to shut off the imagination luring us deeper into the labyrinth of the unknown. Reason converts uncertainty into a definite meaning, and once we know what that meaning is, we don't have to think about it anymore. We can proceed with our task in the specious confidence that this one thing, at least, is solid.

The imagination creates friction with the world by grabbing onto all the objects that go by. It wants to dwell on each one, lovingly or in horror. The ego doesn't bother with trivialities like the connotations of *puto*. The heroic self, impatient to get on with its work, chafes at the imagination which constantly tugs us off on tangents. That is the reason we always move toward our goals far more slowly than we wish. Meanwhile, the soul feels bereaved at the untimely loss of the objects it has been pulled away from. We gain our soul through the friction we experience as we scrape through the phenomena of the physical and human worlds. Keats summarizes this process in a letter to his brother George:

> Call the world if you Please "the vale of Soul-making." Then
> you will find out the use of the world ... How then are Souls to
> be made? How then are these sparks which are God to have
> identity given them—so as ever to possess a bliss peculiar to
> each one's individual existence? How, but by the medium of a
> world like this?[6]

The soul and the world are virtually the same, Keats argues. The individual soul furnishes one particular instance of the vast potentiality of the world. We are each an expression of the world soul at a given place and time. Our soul exists only to the extent that the world has rubbed it into awareness.

The divine resides in everything everywhere although we ourselves may not always be prepared to see it. Like books, any objects in the world project images of themselves, and we apprehend the world by the feelings these object-images arouse. The images of things create a visionary landscape, whose forms and particulars hold up under our utmost demands for meaning.

Here is an example: In December 1962 or January 1963, Beat poet Diane di Prima married Alan Marlowe and decided to move to

Los Angeles, where Alan would pursue an acting career. Di Prima had been away from her home town, New York City, and let a friend live in her apartment there in the meantime. When she returned to pack for the move to Los Angeles, she found "stuff was missing" as she reports in her autobiography *Recollections of My Life as a Woman*:

> I suppose that shouldn't have been a surprise, but it was. The rip-off had been careful—I'd even have to say thoughtful and selective ...
>
> At the time I just noted it, and kept on packing. Maybe a bit faster because of the fury I felt, the betrayal.
>
> What was harder to accept was the non-presence of my small collection of Egyptian scarabs, some old, some new, some probably fakes, of various sizes, colors, and materials. They had been in a box in the top drawer of my dresser, but I found to my sorrow that they were not going to accompany me out West ... Other batches of stuff were missing: Lalique jewelry, and a few things from India and Tibet that Peter Hartman had given me.[7]

Di Prima had grown up in a cold lawyer's household. She had decided early on that she feared poverty less than middle-class conformity. She rejected society's expectations of women by devoting herself to art and ideas. Yet 40 years after the theft, the commune-dwelling, countercultural di Prima reveals that she still misses her stuff, and she takes the loss personally. The things live in her imagination. She can enumerate every piece. She does not miss them for their pecuniary value. She regrets the loss of the fake scarabs as much as the authentic ones, the souvenirs from India and Tibet as much as the Lalique jewelry. I like her wry choice of "non-presence" in the above quote (rather than "absence" or "theft") because the term indicates that the missing things have a life of their own, quite apart from di Prima's possession of them. What made them valuable when di Prima had them and loved them will continue to make them valuable afterward, no matter who has them, and she may console herself with knowing the world has lost nothing even if she herself did.

We don't realize how much we crave it till we find someone who takes "things" seriously. Because she loves things for themselves, di Prima knows what they can do for us. Once we see that things matter to di Prima—not personalities, culture, or history—we notice treasures like this:

> There was a story in my family about my grandmother, Antoinette Mallozzi. For twenty years she had shopped and

done her errands in the same Bronx neighborhood, but one
day she went out and didn't come back for hours. It turned
out there was—or had been—a sign, a woman's boot, that
had hung out over the street to signal the existence of a
cobbler shop. For Antoinette, it also signaled the place where
she had to turn to get home. On this particular day, for whatever reason, the sign was gone: perhaps the shoemaker had
retired or died, perhaps the sign was simply being cleaned. In
any case—no boot, no turn. Antoinette wandered for hours, till
[her husband] Domenico finally found her, not all that far from
her house.[8]

This anecdote is not about di Prima's grandmother or Italian immigrants in the United States. It encapsulates di Prima's philosophy of
meaning: things anchor us to the world. When we lose sight of the
things that constitute the world, we search aimlessly, two steps from
home. I admire di Prima because she knows this unfalteringly. She
does not succumb to the impulse to explain. Her autobiography simply
"re-collects" the things that make up her life because she happens to
know them best.

We experience a text just as we experience anything else in life.
At its most basic level, reading involves collecting or gathering up the
words of a text. Words can be the images of objects, or they can be
objects in themselves. The word "steel" stands for a particular kind of
metal. Yet the word itself has physical properties, an etymology, and a
specific usage; in short, it has its own identity. A word frankly admits
that it is both itself and something else at the same time. Is a text real
or symbolic? Do words refer to something, or do they simply exist?
We cannot escape the ambiguous status of words. In this way, a text
becomes a matrix of uncertainty where the soul can linger. In her epic
Loba, di Prima creates an extensive landscape out of word/things. She
has the eye and hand of a fine artist:

O lost moon sisters
crescent in hair, sea under foot do you wander
in blue veil, in green leaf, in tattered shawl do you wander
with goldleaf skin, with flaming hair do you wander
on Avenue A, on Bleecker Street do you wander
on Rampart Street, on Filmore Street do you wander
with flower wreath, with jeweled breath do you wander ...[9]

Imagine a whole epic made up of passages like this. They describe at
most vague action leading to no definite conclusion. Di Prima does not

impose a plot, character development, or some other logic. Only the refrain "do you wander" hints at the possibility of narrative direction. The less di Prima constrains her words with predicates that aim at a definite goal, the more possibilities they suggest. We do not need to know what "lost moon sisters" or "sea under foot" refers to. They exist as familiar yet strange phrases that inveigle the imagination, juxtapositions of common words that evoke uncommon moods. Merely scraping past these words with our eyes and mind excites meaning.

In this way, the poem becomes a vale of soul-making. The passages in *Loba* exhibit rich details, the fundamental elements of experience. By suppressing the verbs, di Prima has transmuted the nouns and adjectives from transparent linguistic windows onto another realm into real things in their own right, as fixed and refractory as rock. Words become tangible objects. Objects acquire symbolic import. The word "goldleaf" and actual gold leaf exist side by side in this landscape. The word is also a thing, the thing also a sign. Both contribute their quanta of feelings to fashion our existence as souls in the world. They exercise the power to define a part of who we are.

We and things incorporate each other into our life stories as they unfold. We belong to the words we read and the earth we walk on. We become entangled in the landscape that they jointly form. That entanglement is the irreducible experience of meaning. We can't get to the meaning except through the experience. The experience is the meaning. We feel the ghosts and gods of the animate text. We have not simply decoded a message and altered our thinking or empathized with a remote person based on the new information, nor have we read an abstract text that is always and forever the same. We have instead engaged all of our faculties. We heard and smelled as well as thought and felt. We read a particular volume in a particular place at a particular time and responded in a particular way. We assumed its features as our own. We are no longer who we were before. We changed. Reading changed us into the words we encountered on the page and the things they enabled us to feel in the world around us.

NOTES

1 Samuel Taylor Coleridge, "Biographia Literaria," in *The Norton Anthology of English Literature*, vol. 2, ed. M.H. Abrams (New York: W.W. Norton & Company, Inc., 1974), p. 353.
2 Gustave Flaubert, *Trois Contes* (Paris: Garnier-Flammarion, 1965), p. 27.
3 Henry James, *The Golden Bowl* (London: Penguin Books, 1985), p. 470.

4 John Keats, *The Selected Letters of John Keats*, ed. Lionel Trilling (Garden City, NY: Doubleday & Company, Inc. 1951), p. 103.
5 James McCutheon, "A Key Word in Gabriel García Márquez's One Hundred Years of Solitude," *Translation Journal* 13, no. 3 (July 2009) http://translationjournal.net/journal/49garciamarquez.htm.
6 Keats, p. 257.
7 Diane di Prima, *Recollections of My Life as a Woman the New York Years* (New York: Viking Press, 2001), p. 329.
8 Ibid., p. 42.
9 Diane di Prima, *Loba* (New York: Penguin Books, 1998), p. 3.

CHAPTER 7

Consulting oracles

We read for information when we confront a problem with a definite solution. We look at a repair manual when we want to fix our car. We open a cookbook when we need a recipe for chili. We enter our symptoms into a medical website when we feel ill. But we have to read in a different way if we face a problem for which there isn't a ready-made answer: Do I accept a marriage proposal? Do I take a job across the country? Do I reveal a secret I swore to keep? Rational approaches are fruitless. We lie awake at night trying to decide what we really think, what our heart tells us. It tells us contradictory things. We ask advice from friends; we listen carefully to their analysis. It doesn't convince us. We spend days, weeks thinking through all of the benefits and risks of each option. We get out a piece of paper, draw a line down the center, and list the pluses and minuses of our choices. They come out even. We flip a coin. We don't like the result, so we flip again. We're stuck.

When the ancients faced such dilemmas, they resorted to a practice that the Elizabethan poet Sir Philip Sidney describes in *The Defence of Poesy*:

> Among the Romans a poet was called *Vates,* which is as much as a diviner, foreseer, or prophet ... so heavenly a title did that excellent people bestow upon this heart-ravishing knowledge [poetry]. And so far were they carried in their admiration thereof, that they thought in the chanceable hitting upon any of such verses great foretokens of their following fortunes were placed. Whereupon grew the word of *Sortes Virgilianae,* when, by sudden opening Virgil's book, they lighted upon some verse of his ...[1]

Readers in late antiquity and the Middle Ages who were perplexed by a problem would open the *Aeneid* at random, blindly put a finger on a line and try to find in the verse some indication of what to do. The Puritans in seventeenth-century America used the Bible in the same way. People still do it today. In China, people traditionally gathered short and long yarrow stalks. They would hold the yarrow stalks in their hand so that they could not discern the length, and select six stalks one by one and lay them out to form a hexagram. There are 64 possible configurations of longs and shorts. People would then turn to the *I Ching*, an ancient book containing 64 oracles, each corresponding to one of the hexagrams. An oracle consists of several sections of obscure text which people would read through to find an idea that unlocks their problem.

I once experimented with the *I Ching* by flipping six pennies (since I was fresh out of yarrow stalks). Heads equaled a long stalk, tails a short one. At the time, I was trying to decide how ambitious to be with my life. I had recently finished graduate school. I felt empowered by my new skills and ready to tackle a big challenge, but academic jobs, the logical next step, were scarce. Hundreds of applicants competed for each position. A dream I had about this time illustrates the way I felt. I was driving a sleek car with a powerful engine. I was on a one-lane road that wound through fields of deep-green grass beneath old deciduous trees. I was in the middle of a long line of cars moving slowly. I was impatient to get to open road and press the accelerator. I would pull to the left or right to try to pass the cars ahead of me. The sharp curves, thick tree trunks, and close traffic thwarted me every time. So I would meekly return to my place in the line of cars. In my life, I wondered whether I should power ahead with all my energy to achieve fame and success, no matter what wreckage I would create for those around me, or be patient and wait for opportunities to open up for me. I consulted the *I Ching*. The pennies pointed me to hexagram 40, called *hsieh* or "taking apart":

> This hexagram describes your situation in terms of reflection and release from tension. It emphasizes that analyzing and understanding things in order to be delivered from compulsion is the adequate way to handle it. To be in accord with the time, you are told to: take things apart![2]

That seemed a promising start. I needed to escape from my compulsion to speed ahead and instead to make a deliberate decision about my future. Later in hexagram 40, I found:

> Hold-fast(-to)
> Possessing conformity
> Tend-towards
> Small People[3]

At the time, this oracle gave me a clear direction. The *I Ching* counseled me not to try to join the ranks of the important people in my field. I needed to beware of my impulse to zoom ahead. Instead, I should analyze my own situation more. From that moment, I reconciled myself to living a modest life, at least outwardly, and I have sought the company of regular folks—"Small People"—who lack the noise and whoosh of strivers who can so easily disturb one's self-possession. I haven't achieved spectacular success, nor have I crashed. I still have unfulfilled ambitions, as everyone does, yet my life has riches enough to satisfy.

As I read the words of hexagram 40 now, I realize that I could have reached the opposite conclusion. The four lines lack punctuation, so it's not clear how they relate to one another. Suppose I had interpreted "Hold fast(-to)" as referring to my ambition. I could then have read the next three lines as a warning against being too complacent or conventional lest I end up like the "Small People." But I approached the oracle properly. I didn't follow it blindly, nor did I overdetermine what the text means. I allowed myself to project my true feelings into the text. I tried to figure out what the text *could* mean *for me*. The effort of wrestling with the garbled oracle gave me time to imagine a life different from the well-known heroic model of people who pursue money, power, and celebrity.

The practice of consulting oracles looks random or subjective to the rational mind because oracles do not directly address the particular issue facing the questioner. The rational mind conceives of every problem in rational terms. It always points straight ahead. It takes the question literally. It analyzes all relevant factors, gathers information, and tries to calculate the solution. It cannot accept indeterminate problems for which there may be no particular solution or no solution at all.

By contrast, oracles can reveal a good answer even when the question itself is wrong, when it points us in the wrong direction, and we need to pull back and reconsider what the issue really is. One of the questions listed above offers an example of the kinds of issues suitable for an oracle: Do I take a job across the country? Upon reflection, I might ask further: Why did I apply for that job across the country in the first place, or what did managers see in me that they offered me the job? Do I love that kind of work? Did I want to make more money? To boost my ego? Do I want to move there, or am I really trying to get away from something that's bothering me here? What do I envision will happen to me if I move? What will happen if I stay? How will either option affect the direction of my whole life, not just my career? How will it affect my family and friends? When the company first offers the job across country, we may have no idea of all the momentous questions our decision involves, and any of them could stymie us. A one-dimensional method, such as listing pluses and minuses, does not allow room for all the issues to bubble to the surface and for incalculable solutions to emerge. Oracles offer a method for expanding the narrow grounds of the initial question and letting other possibilities into our consciousness. The ancients would have described oracles as creating space for the gods to intervene in our lives.

When we consult an oracle, we always ask a question that implicates ourselves in some way, whether we realize it or not. Therefore, we can easily fall into the trap of interpreting the oracle in the easiest or most favorable light for ourselves so that we miss the deeper, more difficult message we need to hear. Most famously, Herodotus reports that the Lydian king Croesus sent to Delphi to learn whether he should attack Cyrus the Great of Persia. The Pythian priestess at Delphi replied that if Croesus invaded Persia he would destroy a great kingdom. The oracle was fulfilled in an unexpected way. The prideful, overconfident Croesus launched his attack, and Cyrus defeated Croesus and conquered the great kingdom of Lydia.

To avoid Croesus' fate, we need to read the oracle with discipline. The process for consulting an oracle goes like this:

- Ask a question the right way.
- Choose a text based on impulse or attraction.
- Pick out a passage at random.
- Interpret the passage in light of the challenge.

Ask a question the right way. We come to the oracle with a question, but the question itself matters less than our attitude. The question we ask should articulate a challenge that cannot be solved rationally. Most of the problem-solving we do starts with a rational goal. A company executive wants to raise profit margins by two percentage points. A dieter wants to lose 20 pounds. By contrast, we consult an oracle when we don't know what our goal is. We usually realize we don't know where we're going only after a long struggle: We try many times to achieve a goal but fail. We keep switching goals. We achieve a goal but are still not satisfied. Something traumatic in our life disorients us. In any case, we fall into a state of perplexity. Circumstances defeated our straight-ahead, heroic consciousness so that the mind opens to new possibilities. Under these conditions, we don't have to formulate a question for the oracle with great precision. We can bring a narrow, selfish query or a grand, existential one. It doesn't matter. Only the way we listen to the answer matters. The Roman historian Livy tells of three ambassadors returning to Rome from Delphi. They had asked the oracle which of them would become the next king of Rome. The oracle replied that whoever kissed his mother first would rule Rome. When they disembarked from the ship, two of them hastened through the city to their parents, but Lucius Junius Brutus guessed that the oracle referred to the common mother of us all. He dropped to his knees, bent over, and kissed the earth. Brutus would later overthrow Rome's tyrannical king, establish a republic, and become its first consul. The three ambassadors asked the same question and received the same oracle in return. But two leapt to a selfish interpretation while the successful one took a broader view.

Choose a text based on impulse or attraction. We can't go to Delphi to receive an oracle, so we can find one in a book. Almost any text will do. It doesn't have to be a book of oracles like the *I Ching*. We should avoid books that directly relate to our question—for example, a memoir by someone who faced a situation like our own. Rather, a book serves as an arbitrary focus for our attention so that we can work on our problem from a starting point outside the familiar premises that have already led us into a dead end. Thus, we need to choose a text because it caught our eye or captivates us in some way. When Niccolò Machiavelli wanted to write a treatise on power politics, *The Discourses*, he could have turned for inspiration to any number of serious historians from antiquity, such as the realist Thucydides or the cynical Tacitus. Instead, Machiavelli chose Livy, the most provincial of all ancient historians. Furthermore, Machiavelli focused on the first ten books of Livy's chronicle of Rome's rise to world dominance. These books contain mostly myths and legends, starting from Aeneas, who fled after the fall of Troy and came to Italy to found the Roman people. The credulous Livy reports this material in the same level tone with which he later narrates the Punic Wars and other actual events. For example, he describes how Numa, Rome's second king, established its religion:

> ... Numa decided upon a step which he felt would prove
> more effective than anything else [in maintaining the nation's
> morality] with a mob as rough and ignorant as the Romans
> were in those days. This was to inspire them with the fear of
> the gods. Such a sentiment was unlikely to touch them unless
> he first prepared them by inventing some sort of marvellous

> tale; he pretended, therefore, that he was in the habit of
> meeting the goddess Egeria by night, and that it was her
> authority which guided him in the establishment of such rites
> as were most acceptable to the gods and in the appointment
> of priests to serve each particular duty.[4]

The story is ridiculous. Not only would it be impossible for Livy to know what had happened centuries before anyone at Rome kept written records, he explains away the origin of Roman religion as a mere prank. These drawbacks don't faze Machiavelli. He proceeds to draw out political lessons:

> It was religion that facilitated whatever enterprise the senate
> and the great men of Rome designed to undertake. Whoever
> runs through the vast number of exploits performed by the
> people of Rome as a whole, or by many of the Romans indi-
> vidually, will see that its citizens were more afraid of breaking
> an oath than of breaking the law, since they held in higher
> esteem the power of God than the power of man ...
>   It will also be seen by those who pay attention to Roman
> history, how much religion helped in the control of armies,
> in encouraging the plebs, in producing good men, and in
> shaming the bad. So if it were a question of the ruler to whom
> Rome was more indebted, Romulus [the city's founder] or
> Numa, Numa, I think, should easily obtain the first place.[5]

Machiavelli would not have written this handbook on *Realpolitik* unless he had first conceived the possibility in his reading of Livy. Despite the fact that Livy was not the best political historian, Machiavelli read him anyway because somehow it was Livy, rather than anyone else, who stimulated his own thinking. We should follow this line when we choose a book for our oracle. Pick the one that energizes our imagination, not the one we calculate is most relevant.

Pick out a passage at random. An oracle need be only a short passage— even a single sentence will do. An oracle works by giving us a new, unexpected perspective on our problem. To ensure we achieve this perspective, we must not let the subconscious steer us to the passage most likely to address our problem. Accordingly, we need to introduce some randomness in the selection. According to the *Aeneid*, the Cumaean Sybil, who lived in a cave, wrote oracles on leaves. The wind would blow the leaves around, thereby scrambling the message for the recipient. More commonly, ancient oracles were written in oblique language.

For example, hexagram 39 in the *I Ching* advises: "Turning-away necessarily possesses heaviness. Anterior acquiescence has the use-of Limping. Limping implies heaviness indeed."[6] This text doesn't make sense, and that's the point. To use a book for an oracle, we need to pick a passage blindly so that it doesn't make sense. Let a volume fall open by chance; close your eyes and stab the text with your index finger. Or choose a three-digit number and a single-digit number at random; go to the page corresponding to the first number, and count off sentences till you reach the second number. Any method will do as long as it's random.

Interpret the passage in light of the challenge. We must rethink our problem using the terms of the randomly chosen text. But we should not blindly grasp onto the most obvious interpretation. Oracles often seem designed to mislead the recipient. The ancient travel writer Pausanias reports that the people of Messene in the Greek Peloponnese received this oracle from Apollo at Delphi:

> When the he-goat drinks Neda's swirling water,
> I have abandoned Messene: destruction comes.[7]

(IV, 1)

The Messenians spent their energy on keeping he-goats away from the river Neda, but something different fulfilled the prophecy—a weeping fig tree on the river bank whose branches and leaves drooped into the water. The Messenians referred to that species of fig colloquially as a "he-goat." The Spartans invaded Messene, subdued it, and turned the people into serfs. The Messenian community made the mistake of reading the oracle literally rather than contemplating the possible fate hanging over it.

Compare the Messenians' response to that of the Athenians who sent to Delphi for advice about what to do when the Persians invaded Greece in 480 B.C. The Persians' defeat at Marathon ten years earlier made Athens a particular target. Herodotus reports that the oracle said:

> For when other things have been captured, as much as the
>   boundary of Cecrops
> And the sanctuary of most godlike Cithairon hold within them,
> Wide-browed Zeus grants to Tritogeneia that the wooden wall
> Alone remain unplundered, which will benefit you and your
>   offspring.

(VII, 141)

The Athenians debated what these puzzling lines meant. Finally, Themistocles proposed that the "wooden wall" referred to ships. He convinced the Athenians to evacuate their city, get onto boats, and go temporarily to safer locations. The Persians did capture Athens and plunder it, but the Athenians themselves escaped. Shortly afterward, the Athenians used those same ships to defeat the Persian fleet at the battle of Salamis, one of the two great victories that turned back the invasion. The Athenians succeeded because they treated the oracle as an opportunity to let a novel strategy enter into their thinking.

For our own oracle, we must consider every possible connection we can imagine, however absurd, between text and problem. Either one of these interpretations will give us the insight we need, or all of them taken together will point in a certain direction. This exercise forces us to quit the rectilinear perspective of reason and to reorient ourselves obliquely to our problem. Only an unexpected point of view leads to an unexpected solution to our dilemma.

Here let me offer an extended example from my own life to show how the use of books as oracles works. First, the problem: I work full time as a professional writer, and in my spare time, I work on writing books like this one. I have long researched and written material for two or three book projects that I want to complete before I retire. I write to please myself first though I hope others would find them interesting, too. At the same time, I believe that reading and writing prepare us to make a difference in the world at large, and I look for opportunities to demonstrate it. My research into American landscape has given me a little familiarity with architecture and urban design. I wonder whether I should volunteer to help the local preservation society develop a long-term strategy for where to focus its efforts. The society has proven effective and valuable to the community but usually swings into action to save significant buildings only when the wrecking ball threatens them. A long-term strategy would inventory the important structures in the city, create a preservation plan that identifies priorities, and plot out work on these priorities over time rather than reacting to the crisis of the moment. Such a project would provide a valuable service to the community. However, it would also absorb considerable time, probably over many years, and jeopardize the books I'm writing. Which project should I pursue, the one I personally enjoy (writing books) or the one that would serve my community (creating a preservation strategy)?

Next, I pick a text off the top of my head, something I've never read before. I happen to have a copy of Shakespeare's sonnets on the back of a bookshelf. It's been there for 20 years. I was aware of its presence, but I didn't want to read it as I don't particularly care for

Shakespeare. I haven't read his sonnets before, except for a few in other anthologies. Before opening the book, I decide to use Sonnet 100, a nice round number:

Where art thou, Muse, that thou forget'st so long
To speak of that which gives thee all thy might?
Spend'st thou thy fury on some worthless song,
Dark'ning thy pow'r to lend base subjects light?
Return, forgetful Muse, and straight redeem
In gentle numbers time so idly spent,
Sing to the ear that doth thy lays esteem,
And gives thy pen both skill and argument.
Rise, resty Muse, my love's sweet face survey,
If Time have any wrinkle graven there;
If any, be a satire to decay
And make Time's spoils despisèd everywhere.
    Give my love fame faster than Time wastes life;
    So thou prevent'st his scythe and crooked knife.

Next, I need to interpret the sonnet/oracle in light of my problem. I'm afraid of swift and facile work, so I want to take an approach that slows me down and gives me time to meditate on the poem and my dilemma. I will use the eight archetypes of meaning described in Chapter 5 to look at them from several angles. For each archetype, I will first play with the meaning of the text and then apply whatever insight I have gained from it to my problem. To preserve the spontaneity of the exercise, I have kept these interpretations and free associations as I drafted them originally:

Style 1: Depth. We experience depth as being drawn inward into an object, often by layers, where each successive layer feels more significant than the last.

On the surface, Sonnet 100 plays on the classical theme of fame, given by poetry to a lover, as outlasting generations and even other human artifacts. The poet grants a form of eternal life by writing beautifully about whomever he chooses as his subject. His beloved will always remain young and beautiful to those who read his sonnet centuries in the future.

A less obvious layer of meaning indicates that this triumph over time is not absolute. It's more like a race in which the best that the poet can do is keep ahead of time. He implores the Muse: "Give my love fame faster than Time wastes life." The act of writing verse is time-bound; it unfolds within time. The Muse has to "spend time" at it. Indeed, verse itself marks off time. The reference to "numbers" refers to the syllables out of which the poet builds the rhythm of his verse. Things that unfold in time cannot transcend time.

Yet another layer of meaning suggests that the poet cannot tri-umph over time at all. He cannot rely on the Muse on whom he depends because she herself falls victim to time by letting things slip out of her memory: "Where art thou, Muse, that thou forget'st so long ..." The sonnet calls on the Muse and gives the Muse direc-tions, but we do not know whether the Muse returns to the poet as requested. Moreover, the Muse has focused on other things that re-quire "fury" as opposed to "gentle" love poetry. In other words, the Muse has been busy writing about furious clashes between men: bat-tles, political conflicts, personal rivalries—the stuff of history. Kings and generals gain fame because their conflicts determine the fate of nations, and writers celebrate their deeds. The Muse will no doubt lapse back into this subject in the future. A sonnet that seems to exalt love and poetry ultimately concedes that public affairs remain more important.

In respect to my dilemma, Shakespeare's sonnet merely restates my problem. The third level of meaning seems to advise me to work on a preservation strategy for my city, an indisputably important project. Still, the poem does express the writer's longing, if not to defeat time through words, at least to divert the course of events from what it would otherwise be. Writing becomes an experiment in entrepreneur-ship to see what one can make by going against the flow. In defining my problem, then, I have repeated a centuries-old trope. I have got-ten stuck in the life-of-action versus life-of-contemplation dichotomy. Fame doesn't interest me, so the inducement to either kind of life that Shakespeare imagines doesn't apply to my problem. To resolve my di-lemma, I need to formulate the question in a different way. Let me ponder that challenge while I move on to the next archetype.

Favors: Neither

Style 2: Revelation. We experience revelation as the answer to a question that requires hard work to solve.

Let me throw this question out off the top of my head: What is real in Sonnet 100? Real to *me*, something substantial I can use in my own life. So much of the furniture in the poem seems mere literary convention that does not point to any concrete thing in the world. The ostensible focus of the poem, Shakespeare's beloved, barely exists here. What do we learn about her? She (or he) has a "sweet face." That face may or may not have a "wrinkle." She may enjoy the Muse's "lays" unless "the ear" refers to the poet himself or the poet's readership. These vague descriptors convince me that Shakespeare didn't have any particular person in mind. The figure of the beloved serves as an empty literary convention just as the Muse does. It's hard not to see the Muse as a met-aphor for the poet's own inspiration. Shakespeare has been busy writing his historical plays or tragedies. He gets a moment to return to love poetry and wonders aloud whether he's still "got it." Nothing about the Muse suggests an agent independent of Shakespeare. Likewise, he gives his personification of time the conventional literary trappings; "his scythe and crooked knife" refers to the god Chronos (named from the Greek word for time), who used a sickle to kill his father Ouranos (heaven). Not even Shakespeare and his contemporary readers would have responded to these images with more than the satisfaction that readers of mysteries or romances today feel when the novelist merely fulfills the expectations of the genre without adding a new twist.

The language doesn't sound any more real to me than the imagery. The sonnet contains well-worn rhetorical conceits, particularly contraries. The Muse (a daughter of Memory in Greek mythology) is "forgetful." Love poetry gives the Muse "might," whereas epics, tragedies, and histories, traditionally the highest genres, are "worthless," "base," and idle. Yet Shakespeare envisions Time as a warrior who gathers "spoils" from his victims just as the hero of an ancient epic might strip the arms and armor off of a defeated foe. Still, Shakespeare does hit a few clever phrases. I like "be a satire to decay" and "Give my love fame faster than Time wastes life." Although interesting, these sparse expressions don't coalesce into anything; they are the casual off-spring of a playful wordsmith. The verse unwinds fluidly; the sentence structure reads smoothly. Skillful, not extraordinary.

In Sonnet 100, Shakespeare almost seems to have set himself the task of writing a poem about nothing as though to better demonstrate his poetic talent. At bottom, the poem offers a soliloquy on the proper subject of a writer and the goal that the writer strives to reach. Supposedly, writing with "both skill and argument" gives Shakespeare the "might" and "pow'r" to challenge time. He writes for an audience that holds his verse in "esteem." If he chooses the wrong subject, he must "redeem" the misspent time by writing love poems. (Is the metaphor sin or a pawn shop?) This conflict doesn't trouble Shakespeare very much, though, because he switches between genres readily. The business about the forgetful Muse comes across as an indirect boast about his versatility. This view of Sonnet 100 does apply to me as a writer because I also wonder what my proper subject is. However, I do not possess Shakespeare's facility with many genres. I cannot switch writing tasks with a simple invocation of the muse. Therefore, maybe I should reformulate my problem like this: Do I have the talent to switch back and forth between writing and a new enterprise (creating a preservation strategy)?

Favors: Neither

Style 3: Recognition. We experience recognition when we discover something about ourselves or others that we knew all along but didn't acknowledge.

I recognize in Sonnet 100 Shakespeare the nihilist, whom I have also found in the tragedies. The slaughter and devastation that cap the action of plays such as *Hamlet* and *Macbeth* argue for a bleak appraisal of human possibilities by Shakespeare. Characters seem unable to understand what's going on around them or to rein in the bestial impulses that issue in killings. Shakespeare never seems to imagine a character as smart as himself. It's as if, with a sweep of his hand, he consigns the whole lot of us to irredeemable failure. The sonnet doesn't contain slaughter, but the same emptiness lies at the heart. The poem contains nothing real except Shakespeare himself. He believes in his own talent, nothing else. The world at large remains empty in his imagination. He populates Sonnet 100 only with well-worn poetic tropes, the bare minimum of furniture which a poet needs to do his work.

I do not want to be a virtuoso like that. I want my writing to open the world for readers. I see words as living objects in the world and the writer's task as enriching the reader's understanding and giving him new capabilities. I would like to think that my readers can create more with what I furnish them than I can myself. This credo suggests that I need to continue to focus on my writing rather than switch to a preservation project in which writing would be ancillary to a more visible, uncomfortable role.

Favors: Writing

Style 4: Boundary-crossing. We experience boundary-crossing when someone pushes through an assumed limit into an area with different rules.

Shakespeare crosses a boundary when he switches from one genre (history plays or tragedies) to another (love lyrics). The transition does not convey tremendous significance because we learn so little about the rules of the first genre. A 14-line poem lacks space for lengthy descriptions, so we must settle for cryptic allusion. Nor do we learn much about how Shakespeare himself managed the transition. How did he cross the boundary? Sonnet 100 provides one clue: when the Muse was busy with genre 1, she was asleep or at least lying down at rest from the point of view of genre 2. Perhaps Shakespeare dreamed about love and love poetry while he wrote his plays. The imagery of love came alive in his sleep. It engaged his libido. He wrote verse in his dreams. He possessed a reserve of creative energy that he could tap into when he had an opportunity to write sonnets again.

My dilemma creates a similar situation. As a writer, I pursue writing as my waking avocation. I have devoted 35 years to thinking about writing and practicing the craft. Now I contemplate switching "genres" to creating a long-term preservation strategy for my city. I believe I have the skills to carry it through, but do I have a reserve of creative energy for it? Do I dream about architecture and preservation at night? The answer is not very much. Without that energy, the work would become a slog. Although my intellect sees the value of it, my heart would not support me halfway through such a long, complex project. Perhaps, my mind will change eventually. Until then, I would only cause people aggravation if I forced myself to start work on something I would abandon in the middle or struggle through without inspiration.

Favors: Writing

Style 5: Novelty. We experience novelty as the sudden appearance of something we never imagined existing or being possible.

I mentioned that I liked some novel turns of phrase in Sonnet 100. If Shakespeare's love has a wrinkle, "be a satire to decay," he tells the Muse. The phrase attracts attention because it doesn't quite fit. The word "satire" sticks out. We expect an adverb rather than a noun, for example, "help me write *satirically* about decay." After all, the Muse is Shakespeare's inspiration, but the noun suggests that Shakespeare refers to Sonnet 100 itself—a poem could be a satire. Even so, a sonnet, whose proper subject is love, cannot be a satire; they are two different genres.

"Satire" could mean "make fun of" (though this definition of satire is imprecise).Therefore, Shakespeare's telescoped, four-word phrase might mean that the fame and beauty of his love, preserved forever through the poem, demonstrates the impotence of time and decay, which otherwise boast their invincibility.

More precisely, the word satire comes from the Greek "satyr," a mythical figure, half man, half goat, who featured in satyr plays. Actors presented a satyr play in the evening as comic relief for the audience after a set of three tragedies in the morning and afternoon. Satyr plays exaggerated the foibles of the gods and heroes in Greek mythology for comic effect. Oversexed satyrs added to the mayhem on stage. Perhaps, Shakespeare envisioned the sonnet as a kind of satyr play to the tragedies he alludes to writing at the beginning. This interpretation makes less sense in that Sonnet 100 doesn't contain the exaggeration for comic effect that we expect of satire.

Shakespeare's choice of "satire" is off just enough to suggest multiple interpretations yet still close enough that we find it meaningful rather than confusing. Young writers often try to pull off this kind of trick without success. They lack the talent for subtle handling that Shakespeare displays here. I personally don't care for such word play and never employ it in my own work. As a writer, though, I admire word skill in any form. Seeing what Shakespeare can do, his cleverness with language makes me wonder whether I pack enough meaning into my own sentences. I worry that I choose colorless expressions. I have more to learn and more to achieve as a writer. I should stick to practicing this craft instead of switching to a different task.

Favors: Writing

Style 6: Beauty. We experience beauty as the arrangement of parts into definite forms.

Sonnets require us to read with a double consciousness. First, they present an explanation of something in a series of sentences whose patterns vary from sonnet to sonnet. The poet constructs this rhetoric to suit the particular topic and mood of each sonnet, which, therefore, has a unique trajectory. Second, sonnets follow a strict rhythmic pattern. The Shakespearean sonnet comprises three quatrains in an ABAB rhyme scheme and a rhyming couplet. The iambic pentameter lines alternate unstressed and stressed syllables, without much variation. Therefore, the reader knows the sonnet has a life span of just 14 lines and 140 syllables, which tick off with the regularity and inevitability of a clock. At least subconsciously, we know at every point exactly how much "life" remains in the sonnet. These two strands, rhetoric and rhythm, unfold in our minds simultaneously as we read the text. We follow them to see whether the sonnet makes much or little of its fixed amount of time. Naturally, the poet tries to pack as much as possible into the short space of a sonnet. Thus, this poetic form lends itself to a heightening of thought and imagination. We can't resist the elegance of a well-written sonnet, such as Sonnet 100.

Great architecture does the same kind of thing. The architect starts with a fixed amount of space, namely, a building lot of a certain dimension plus the setbacks and other restrictions imposed by the zoning code. The architect then uses the syntax of structure and style to develop a unique expression for the building. If the architecture is good, each vantage point from which we look at the building conveys a decisive feeling. Inside, the building flows from room to room in a certain way. The occupant takes pleasure in deciphering—perhaps over years—the forms that the architect has created.

Should I spend my time showing people the beauty of poems or the beauty of my city's architecture? I enjoy poetry myself, but I do not want to "teach" literature. Moreover, poetry is a solitary hobby that appeals to few people. By contrast, almost everyone loves touring interesting buildings. The people of my city could better appreciate the extraordinary architecture that surrounds them. Any building project depends to some degree on public opinion. A better informed public would push developers to go to the expense of rehabbing great buildings rather than tearing them down or to invest in great architecture for new buildings rather than settling for generic designs that detract from the neighborhood. Creating a preservation strategy would serve to educate the public about the great buildings in its midst, a more worthy goal than writing about literature.

Favors: Preservation

Style 7: Order. We experience order as the logical connection between parts to form a larger, coherent system.

Sonnets are long enough to develop complex thoughts, short enough for us to read at the highest pitch of attention. Their structure keeps us oriented so that we can concentrate on the text. The four parts of a Shakespearean sonnet develop an argument in a classic narrative arc: situation, rising action, climax, and denouement. Each quatrain comprises one complete sentence. The story builds in three equal rhetorical steps. In Sonnet 100, the first quatrain sets up the situation by upbraiding the Muse. The second one recalls the Muse to her proper task, and the third gives her specific instructions. The couplet provides a quick, satisfying resolution by stating the bottom line—stop time's "scythe and crooked knife." The structure of the sonnet creates simplicity out of complexity. After all, Shakespeare juggles a number of difficult problems at the same time: switching from one genre to another, determining which genre is more important, counteracting the destructive power of time, and so on. The poet can impose some order on this material simply by pouring it into the sonnet form. This template forces him to complete a thought every four lines, and he has to summarize everything in a rhyming couplet, a common verse form for rational discourse.

Similarly, great architecture creates order out of its surroundings. For example, an attractive entry can invite passersby to come inside. Buildings sited properly in relation to one another on a campus can create walk paths that crisscross and lead to casual meetings. Thus, the architecture reinforces the community. A beautiful elevation or façade induces other builders to invest in design to live up to that standard so that the whole neighborhood improves. By contrast, a poorly designed building leaves holes in its surroundings. For example, all too often we see nice rows of storefronts interrupted by a plaza or gas station with a wide parking lot in front. People who would otherwise continue window shopping decide instead to turn around or cross the street rather than enter the void that the parking lot creates on the street. Walkable neighborhoods in cities and villages face constant threats from developers who cut corners on design or want to accommodate motorists at the expense of the street. A preservation strategy would identify the key architectural points that turn mere streets into walkable, human-scale neighborhoods. A preservation strategy benefits the whole city for generations. By contrast, a book helps one person at a time and delivers uncertain long-term benefits.

Favors: Preservation

Style 8: Tradition. We experience tradition as a sense of continuity over time.

We can gain insight from a text by looking at similar kinds of works that have come before. Shakespeare came in a long line of poets who wrote sonnet cycles. After a quick look through one of these cycles, Philip Sidney's *Astrophel and Stella,* I found this sonnet (no. 70), which addresses some of the same themes in Shakespeare's Sonnet 100, including the limits of poetry:

> My Muse may well grudge at my heavenly joy
> If still I force her in sad rhymes to creep.
> She oft hath drunk my tears, now hopes to enjoy
> Nectar of mirth, since I Jove's cup do keep.
> Sonnets be not bound prentice to annoy;
> Trebles sing high, as well as basses deep;
> Grief but Love's winter livery is; the boy
> Hath cheeks to smile as well as eyes to weep.
> Come then, my Muse, show thou height of delight
> In well-rais'd notes; my pen, the best it may,
> Shall paint out joy, though but in black and white.
> Cease, eager Muse; peace, pen, for my sake stay.
> I give you here my hand for truth of this:
> Wise silence is best music unto bliss.

Sidney wrings amusement out of the tradition of poets who complain endlessly about the torments of love yet never get around to its pleasures. He wants to write about the joy—"Sonnets be not bound prentice to annoy"—but his Muse resists. He resorts to reason or analogies to make his point: "Trebles sing high, as well as basses deep." Like Shakespeare, Sidney exhorts his Muse: "show thou height of delight." But he throws up his hands abruptly in the last three lines. Just stop, already, Sidney seems to plead. Let me enjoy my bliss in "wise silence."

When you put Sidney's sonnet next to Sonnet 100, certain qualities of Shakespeare's stand out. Shakespeare is a smoother, clearer writer than Sidney, whose expressions often sound crabbed, even Yoda-like: "Grief but Love's winter livery is." At times, Sidney strains to fill lines as in the almost throwaway parenthetical phrase in the second half of this one: "Shall paint out joy, though but in black and white." By contrast, Shakespeare puts every syllable of his sonnet to good use. However, Shakespeare comes across as a cold, ambitious writer in Sonnet 100, compared to the more humane Sidney. Sidney acknowledges other interests in life besides writing. At a certain point, he willingly lays his pen aside to pursue them. Sidney has more fun with his sonnet. Instead of a conceit carried through from start to finish, Sidney grabs at metaphors on the fly almost for the amusement of stretching his diction as far as it will go: "creep," "nectar," "prentice," "trebles," and so on. Whereas Shakespeare's Muse is his own inspiration, Sidney's Muse is a straight man, the target of the poet's sallies.

Viewing Sonnet 100 from the perspective of tradition doesn't much help me decide whether to continue to focus on my writing or work on the preservation strategy. Comparing two styles always makes me wonder whether I can apply any tricks I spot to my own writing. I tend more to the sleek, professional Shakespeare style, but the exuberance of the Sidney style appeals to me also. How could I add some of it to my prose? To apply an architectural analogy, Sonnet 100 reminds me of a Frank Lloyd Wright house—modern and ingenious but too dark and cold to live in comfortably. I'd much rather live in a warmer, more exuberant house designed by McKim, Mead, and White. A preservation strategy has room for both kinds of houses. So tradition tips toward writing only a little.

Favors: Writing

At the end of my eight excurses, I have decided to devote myself to writing and forget about the preservation strategy. Writing came out on top in four of the eight excurses, with two pointing toward the preservation strategy and two neutral. More importantly, the tenor of these interpretations reminds me of my own character. I have a moderate temperament. I am not driven to piling up achievements or building a reputation. I prefer to choose a goal from personal interest and pursue it with steady passion. I am capable of doing many things, including some with a serious public purpose such as creating a preservation strategy. Nevertheless, if the excitement isn't deeply rooted, my commitment will peter out. I know I have a sustained passion for writing, whereas a preservation strategy is a good idea but not an idea specifically for me.

I wrote the eight excurses on Sonnet 100 ad hoc as their uneven quality reveals. In rereading them, their applications to my dilemma seem arbitrary. Nevertheless, the interpretations accurately reflect my thoughts at the time of writing, especially no. 4, boundary-crossing. If I were to come back to the poem at a later time or with a different problem, I would write different excurses. Some of the excurses show a little insight and creativity; others are pale and forced. Yet the quality of my literary criticism does not correlate to the degree of conviction I have in the answers to the writing versus preservation question. A bad interpretation of the text/oracle can just as easily lead to a solution as a good interpretation. Indeed, I did not write the excurses to explore Sonnet 100 in a disciplined, analytical way. I wrote them as experiments to see what light I could shed on my own dilemma. In some cases, the experiment failed; in others, it succeeded. I do not need to be inspired at every point. I need just enough inspiration to make a decision or attain more clarity. After all, that is why one consults an oracle—or reads, for that matter.

NOTES

1 Sir Philip Sidney, *Selected Prose and Poetry*, ed. Robert Kimbrough (New York: Holt, Rinehart and Winston, Inc., 1969), p. 106.
2 *I Ching: The Classic Chinese Oracle of Change*, trs. Rudolf Ritsema and Stephen Karcher (New York: Barnes & Noble Books, 1995), p. 444.
3 Ibid., pp. 451–2.
4 Titus Livy, *The Early History of Rome*, tr. Aubrey de Selincourt (New York: Penguin Books, 1960), p. 54 (I,19).
5 Niccolò Machiavelli, *The Discourses*, tr. Leslie J. Walker (London: Penguin Books, 1983), pp. 139–40.
6 *I Ching*, p. 436.
7 Pausanias, *Guide to Greece, vol. 2 Southern Greece* (London: Penguin Books, 1988), p. 148.

CHAPTER 8

Translation

Words contain a motive power that even dedicated readers under-
estimate. We can see it more clearly if we go back to the early days
of reading. Thousands of years ago, when writing was still new,
people considered reading a mystical activity. By reading, one could
recover ideas in their primeval form as the gods first uttered them to
mankind. Reading must have seemed as miraculous to the Sumerians
and Babylonians as it would to us if we were somehow to discover the
vocabulary list that Adam made when he denominated all the parts
of creation.

The ancients considered writing simply a device that recorded
a speaker's voice, and the reader reenacted that voice for himself as
he sounded out the words. For example, after Hammurapi, the king
of Babylon (1792–1749 B.C.), conquered his empire, he wrote a legal code so that the many different peoples he ruled would enjoy the
same laws. For the first time, the law was imagined as a universal idea,
applying equally to everyone everywhere, not just as a set of customs
handed down in the particular location where one happened to be
born. Hammurapi inscribed his code on a seven-foot, black diorite
pillar or stele. This very stele stands today in the Louvre Museum in
Paris. Visitors can walk around it and even touch it if not for the low
warning ropes. Its topmost quarter contains a relief sculpture showing
king Hammurapi standing before an enthroned Shamash, the deity
who gave him the laws and commissioned him to establish justice on
earth. Solar rays rise from the shoulders of Shamash, god of the Sun as
well as Justice. By reading the text carved into the stele, a Babylonian
could literally hear the voice of Shamash himself, handed on through
Hammurapi, as if he were speaking at that moment for the first time.
The epilogue of the Law Code of Hammurapi reads:

Let the wronged man who has a case go before my statue
called "King of Justice" and read out my inscribed stele and
hear my valuable words. Let my stele illuminate for him the
case, so that he will discover his rights and appease his
heart.[1]

The act of reading opens a portal to the realm of the gods. We return
to a primitive experience of the world. In the instant we confront a
text, we become receptive to the god. We anticipate his divinity. We
don't yet know what he will say to us or what will happen to us after
we have read. Everything seems possible during this moment while the
god is determining what he will say. We begin reading. For as long as
we read, his voice resonates in us. We feel his vibrations deep in our
chest. When the text ends and the god's voice dies away, a consciousness of the laws and the fate he has pronounced for us becomes fixed,
irrevocable. Through words, the god has intervened to alter our life.

Words move us so profoundly because they are what turn ideas into
a lived experience. For this reason, ancient readers did not draw sharp
distinctions between an author's text and his meaning. When readers
pondered an author's thought what they pondered was his text, his
words. You could not know an author unless you had read what he had
actually written. As its most basic method, Greek and Roman education required the memorization and recital of Homer and Vergil. Every
literate person knew these texts by heart. They could quote the *Odyssey*
and *Aeneid* at length from memory. The expressions and rhetorical
tropes in these works furnished a stock of tools that readers could apply
in any circumstances. The ancients lived in the verbal universe that
had sprung out of these texts. Poetry, philosophy, rhetoric, art, history,
and so on—most of the riches of ancient culture owe something to the
words of Homer and Vergil.

The Dark Ages created the conditions for the development of our
modern conception of reading, one in which words and meaning are
distinct. By the ninth century, Latin had unstuck from the speech of
daily life. Any secular reading public had evaporated. Only the top
churchmen and government officials could read and write. A small
group of educated people scattered across Europe wrote for each other
on intellectual subjects in Latin. And they had learned to do so silently,
as though communing with God in the privacy of their own minds.

Scholastic theology emerged from this environment in the elev-
enth century. The scholastics adopted the syllogism and classification
to analyze theological problems. Theologians sifted through the received wisdom of the early church fathers, such as Origen, Jerome,

and Augustine, who lay closer in time to Jesus and were supposedly inspired by God. But their voluminous works contained contradictions, differing explanations for points of doctrine, and gaps where the church fathers hadn't addressed issues that had occurred to later readers. The scholastics believed that people of today could derive more accurate answers to theological questions by reasoning through the issues for themselves. The instrument of logic would allow the scholastics to see God's meaning directly rather than at second hand through the mediation of the church fathers.

Anselm from Canterbury, England, one of scholasticism's founders, devised his famous ontological proof of God's existence at this time. The following passage from Anselm's *Proslogium*, written in 1077, gives the flavor of this proof and of scholastic thought in general. It takes the form of a prayer:

> And so, Lord, do thou, who dost give understanding to faith, give me, so far as thou knowest it to be profitable, to understand that thou art as we believe; and that thou art that which we believe. And, indeed, we believe that thou art a being than which nothing greater can be conceived ... And whatever is understood, exists in the understanding. And assuredly that, than which nothing greater can be conceived, cannot exist in the understanding alone. For, suppose it exists in the understanding alone: then it can be conceived to exist in reality; which is greater.
>
> Therefore, if that, than which nothing greater can be conceived, exists in the understanding alone, the very being, than which nothing greater can be conceived, is one, than which a greater can be conceived. But obviously this is impossible. Hence, there is no doubt that there exists a being, than which nothing greater can be conceived, and it exists both in the understanding and in reality.[2]

For the scholastics, God was logic itself, and one could move nearer to God only through the use of logic to contemplate him in his true nature. They did not want simply to believe what some ancient authority said about God but "to *understand* that thou art as we believe" through the use of reason. The scholastics felt a thrill of power to consider that they could fathom the deepest secrets of God and the universe through intellectual rigor alone. They didn't have to go anywhere or talk to anyone to make discoveries; they could do it sitting in a chair by themselves.

Logic alone cannot save Anselm's proof from the arbitrariness of its premises. The proof begins: "we believe that thou art a being than which nothing greater can be conceived." Christians believe this; others do not. If Anselm wants to demonstrate God's existence through airtight logic, he first needs to prove that Christian belief is the right entry point for his argument. Christians also believe many other things about God beside his greatness—why start with that particular attribute rather than, say, God's omniscience or his love? Anselm papers over these gaps in his reasoning with word play. Language allows us to say that something "exists" in the understanding and something "exists" in reality, yet the two things do not exist in the same way. We cannot compare these two forms of existence and say that one is greater than the other any more than we can say the number 4 is greater than an apple. Anselm's "proof" amounts to arguing that God must exist simply because we believe it.

However, Anselm's language has the familiar ring of the precise, step-by-step analytical writing of today. Scholars in the sciences, social sciences, and humanities practice it within academic publications; legal, medical, and other professions employ the style as well, along with analysts in think tanks and research firms. Anselm cuts the prose into clear segments of thought. Each clause expresses a simple, distinct idea. Each sentence appears irrefutable at first. Together, they form a chain of reasoning that produces what seems an inescapable conclusion.

Anselm means the reader to stop after each sentence if necessary to make sure he fully understands the point before proceeding to the next one. For Anselm, the reader dwells in heaven to the extent that his mind grasps the eternal principles that rule everything. Thus, Anselm defines every nuance in his argument with precision even if doing so makes the sentences laborious: "Therefore, if that, than which nothing greater can be conceived, exists in the understanding alone, the very being, than which nothing greater can be conceived, is one, than which a greater can be conceived." A prose stylist would never repeat such an awkward phrase three times in one sentence, but Anselm prefers to overdetermine his language than allow any opportunity for doubt about his meaning.

Anselm's style of thinking and writing is one result of the severing of Latin from common speech, according to Erich Auerbach:

> The dialectical, scientific Latin of scholasticism developed
> in a direction contrary to humanistic rhetoric. Scholasticism
> exerted a revolutionary effect on the language, for, breaking
> drastically with the tradition of literary Latin, which had

hitherto been essentially rhetorical and even manneris-
tic, it concentrated for the first time on scientific accuracy.
For scientific purposes the isolation of medieval Latin from
everyday usage proved to be a significant advantage.
This circumstance—the freedom of words from current
associations—made it relatively easy for theology and philosophy (as well as jurisprudence, which, to be sure, had a tradition to refer back to) to create a clear and precise language
in which to express their specialized concepts. This of course
required the use of neologisms which sounded barbarous to
the classically trained ear and the abandonment of the har-
monious sentence structure of classical rhetoric. But the great
achievements of scholastic logic, its combination and creation
of ideas, would not have been possible without such an
instrument; and such an instrument could have developed at
that time only on the basis of a pre-existing written language
distinct from the spoken tongue.[3]

The scholastics did not view their intellectual work as occurring
within a living community which has a history and specific concerns
and which continues to develop and change. Scholastic theology deliberately stands apart from the world. Therefore, Anselm and his peers
sought not a "dead" language, as Latin is often called but an eternal,
unchanging language. They aspired to the authority of heaven.

Anselm's style of writing altered the relationship between text
and meaning that the ancients assumed with Homer and Vergil. For
Anselm and the scholastics, the text has unhooked from the argument
it expresses. To know Anselm, you don't need to know his text—you
don't even need to have read it at all. All you need to do is to grasp
his logic, that is, the abstract steps of reasoning that lead up to his
conclusion. Thus, a philosopher or theologian could legitimately learn
Anselm's ontological proof from a secondary source and then write his
own critique of that proof without ever having seen Anselm's actual
words. Indeed, Anselm's original words fell into disuse even though
the ontological proof and his fame endured. "In Anselm's own lifetime," writes Charles Hartshorne:

a tradition—we may call it "the Gaunilo tradition," since [this
opponent of Anselm] is its founder—began to take shape that
one scarcely reads Anselm: rather one refutes him essentially
unread, so decisively that reading him would be needless
toil. Only upon the assumption that the great majority of

commentators upon the Argument which Anselm invented
have viewed the original exposition almost entirely at second-
hand can it be explained that what Anselm evidently thought
were his most important points are left without even a men-
tion, not only in the most widely-cited refutations, but also in
some of the better known defenses.[4]

The lack of respect for Anselm's text is inherent to the scholastics' approach to knowledge. The text ceases to matter as a valuable object in itself and serves, insofar as it cannot be dispensed with, as a mere vehicle for conveying the original logical proposition. Language becomes a medium of communication rather than divine speech channeled through the reader's voice. Once the argument is launched into the world, the text in which it first appeared becomes unnecessary. Philosophers could quarrel with or improve on Anselm's argument, using more precise distinctions to express these thoughts, without being tied to Anselm's words.

Thus, the scholastics scarcely heeded the art and performance of language, such as we saw with Hammurapi's stele and other ancient books. The text plays a similarly utilitarian role in many publications today. Analytic writing presents arguments that can be evaluated apart from the words. Journalism and textbooks convey information in workmanlike prose. Biographies and cheap fiction deliver stories without the text needing to be studied closely. The writer creates the text to convey a meaning. The meaning exists outside of the text in the insubstantial realm of pure thought. The text serves as a kind of syringe that can be discarded as soon as the meaning is injected into us. We do not reenact and participate in the writer's ideas the way readers of Hammurapi's stele did. Instead, we receive those ideas passively because they are relayed from an abstract authority. The author only expects us to think about them.

We inscribe this deference to the writer's authority in a common assumption about language, which Ludwig Wittgenstein conveniently summarizes: "Every word has a meaning. The meaning is correlated with the word. It is the object for which the word stands."[5] The formula seems so simple as to be undeniable. It aligns three terms: word, meaning, and object. It implies a one-to-one correspondence between word and meaning. Each word has "a meaning," one meaning. The word and its meaning are "correlated," that is, some arbitrary assignment has been made so that all speakers of a language understand that a particular word corresponds to a particular meaning. That meaning points to an "object" in the world, whether concrete or conceptual. Thus, the use of a given word by the speaker or writer compels us readers or listeners ineluctably toward some specific thing. Since the writer chooses the words in the text, he also controls the meaning and where in the world it leads. The reader can only go along for the ride to its predetermined destination. If a writer uses the word "tree," I must admit I know the reality to which he refers. I can't avoid it or argue around it without being dishonest.

The printed page furthers this fatalistic notion of meaning. In print, each sentence seems to have reached its eternal form. The writing seems decisive—precisely these words and no others, with no afterthoughts. But this view of writing's permanence and authority is an optical illusion. Writers are no more settled or decisive than readers.

By the time I finish writing this sentence, it will change.

Like any writer, I constantly reconsider what I want to say and so edit and reedit the text as I compose it. I play around with various wordings in my head, and I commit the most promising ones to the page. I arrange and rearrange words on the screen. I prune them. I make substitutions. I think about the rhythm and where the punctuation should go. Each change to the text introduces subtle shifts in emphasis. Thus, even a simple sentence such as the one in italics above goes through many permutations, each with its own nuance. For example, to stress that the writing of the sentence extends over time, I first wrote, "By the time I get to the end ..." I tried making the thought impersonal by substituting "the writer" for "I." I even considered being dogmatic: "Sentences change as they are being written."

For a writer, the process of composing and editing sentences never ends. Therefore, the sentence reaches a series of ends:

- When I conceive of the sentence in my head
- When I first commit it to paper
- After each revision
- When I give a copy to peer reviewers
- After I revise the text based on their feedback
- When I deliver the manuscript to the publisher
- When I make the revisions that the editor suggests
- When I make changes suggested by the copyeditor
- When the sentence is finally published

The sentence assumes a final, immobile form simply because of the medium in which it appears and not because I have finished thinking about it or considered all possible versions. At any point in the long process of writing a sentence, I could have made a different choice that would have changed the way it appears in print. Even after publication, my internal editor does not stop. Sentences haunt my mind, and I think, "That sentence doesn't quite work. If I'd written it this way, I could have conjured a richer meaning." Most of the time, sentences mercifully fade from my memory so that their evolution reaches no decisive conclusion but merely peters out.

The act of publication cuts off the development of sentences arbitrarily. They remain fixed in that moment of time. The reader receives this frozen uncertainty in the form of a text. Nevertheless, we expect the reader to respect all of its sentences as authoritative, as if fully intended by the writer.

Creative readers allow themselves as much flexibility to generate meaning from a text as the author enjoyed when he composed it. To do so, we need a less rigid theory of language than the utilitarian one Wittgenstein summarizes above. In *The Banquet*, Dante says that "words are made to reveal what is not known."[6] He emphasizes the *uses* of language rather than the transaction between writer and reader. Language involves an act of creation—"words are made"— perhaps by a writer or speaker, perhaps by a reader or listener. Dante does not specify which. The Latin original for "are made," *facta sunt*, can also mean "become" or "come into being." Words seem to spring into existence miraculously and, therefore, hearken back to the genesis of the world, to the Adamic moment when language makes our surroundings tractable. Words tell us little about their author or his intention. Instead, they exist to serve a purpose, that is, to "reveal" something. Words perform their crucial function during that instant when they disclose an unexpected meaning. At the decisive moment, something new arrives in our consciousness. Intellectual energy thrills through us. Words properly convey something striking if not life-changing. The mere description of facts does not interest Dante at all. The correlation of "tree" with its meaning and its object leaves us no wiser about the world. Dante removes the arbitrary association of word and meaning from the equation. He views words and objects as identical. They are undifferentiable. They form a single experience. The reader's experience of the word *is* his experience of the object. The object arrives in our consciousness as its name. The object is the word. The deictic function of language does not apply. A word no longer points to an object separate from it in fact and nature. The two are merged in the preconscious realm. Dante's use of the present tense—"what is not known"—suggests that the object never becomes fully known. Language does not convey perfect knowledge.

Words deliver revelations because they are not static counters that each stand for something specific. Rather, each word comprises several meanings along historical, cultural, and linguistic dimensions. A word functions more like a node in a network of meanings that can take readers in any number of directions. Let's go back to "tree." If we follow the conventional formula Wittgenstein summarizes, we must decode the word. When we see the word "tree," we associate it with the botanical phenomenon tree. The letters t-r-e-e are the cipher for an actual tree. To read in a given language, we need to learn its pairing of words and concepts. *Arbor* means tree in Latin, *dendron* in Greek, and *Baum* in German. The various languages represent the same class of plant by different collections of symbols, which have been correlated with it by long convention. We, therefore, assume that *tree, arbor, dendron,* and *Baum* are equivalent and mean the same thing.

Indeed, they come close, but they don't substitute for one another perfectly. Each word acquires a unique range of meaning, based on the lived experience of the people who speak the language. To a Roman, *arbor* did not mean precisely the same things that "tree" means to us. The species of trees that we have in northern climates and to which we apply the word "tree" differ from the Mediterranean species for which a Latin speaker would use *arbor*. For example, a Latin speaker would class the arbutus and short varieties of cypress as *arbores*, whereas English speakers would call them "bushes" or "shrubs." A Greek often chose *dendron* to refer to trees that bear fruit and nuts as well as to shrubs; he would use a different word, *hyle*, to describe tall trees used for timber. In German, *Baum* can mean mast, pole, or rafter as well as tall trees, but not shrubs.

Each word possesses several meanings, and it typically appears in a text in relationship to certain other words that color its meaning in various ways. Every word in a language conveys a unique set of associations to the reader based on the contexts in which it is used. In a particular context, one sense of the word predominates, but the other associations lurk in the background. The reader hears them as overtones, which shape his experience of the text. If we come across the word *ferrum* in a Latin text, we go to our Latin-English dictionary, and we discover that it means "iron." We think we know exactly what the word means because we have found an equivalent word in English. When we become more proficient in Latin, we realize that *ferrum* conveys a different sensibility than iron does in English. *Ferrum* most often has the extended meaning of "sword." Thus, the word nearly always dyes the text with some martial tinge even when *ferrum* just refers to the metal. The extended meaning of the English word "iron" is a device for smoothing the wrinkles out of clothes or perhaps a tool used to maneuver wood in a fireplace. "Iron" implies a domestic or possibly industrial sensibility. *Ferrum* doesn't mean iron, after all. *Ferrum* can only mean *ferrum*, with the particular set of references and implications it acquires when set within Latin texts. It conveys not only a general idea but also untranslatable connotations that only people who speak the language grasp. The reader hears all of these nuances in the word even when one denotation is prominent.

Every word heads off in multiple directions that link it tentatively to other ideas. We start looking for confirmation of those ideas in the nuances of other words, so one word sparks a chain reaction in our imagination. This polyvalence of words gives a text its suggestive, dreamlike character. We grasp these possibilities intuitively while the rational mind shines its solar rays on the writer's intended meaning. Indeed, the most powerful abilities we bring to the text reside in our unconscious. Just as our cerebellum elegantly controls our physical actions without us having to think about them, some part of the brain functions automatically when we read a text. Reading often seems effortless even as our brain performs complex functions.

We glimpse some of this submerged work when we start to learn a language and have to think through sentences painfully. Reading then unfolds in slow motion. It gives us an opportunity to examine the operations our mind performs, which occur too swiftly to appreciate when we read in our native tongue. I hold a book of Italian short stories in my right hand. An Italian-English dictionary lies open to my left. I read the text of a story sentence by sentence, looking up words as I go:

> Si somigliano, sembrano gentili, hanno lentiggini sulle guance, sorridono, qualcuno con la bocca sporca di more.[7]

I spot four third-person plural verbs in the present indicative tense. I see no plural subject, so it must be an unexpressed "they." I look up "somigliano." I look up "lentiggini." I look up "guance." I look up "more." "Si" is a reflexive pronoun. "Gentili" is a predicate adjective. "Lentiggini" is a direct object. "Qualcuno" begins a phrase in apposition to the subject. I experience the satisfaction that comes from piecing together the syntax of a complete sentence. I pause. I want to move onto the next sentence. But I have forgotten what *lentiggini* means although I looked it up 30 seconds before. It is a key word of the sentence, a vivid detail about all of the figures in the story, and the author wants readers to notice it: "They look alike, they seem nice, they have _____ on their cheeks, they smile, one with his mouth stained from mulberries." I must look up *lentiggini* again. It means "freckles."

As I read in a language that is new to me, I experience the foreboding of a horror film. Every ordinary word suggests more than appears on the surface. I ask myself whether the description marks the children as normal or abnormal. Do the *lentiggini* lend them charm or disfigure them? Does *la bocca sporca di more* indicate a ravenous appetite that will soon turn on the narrator? Are they all alike in the freshness of youth or in their bestiality? Such is the primeval force of language that words excite or disorient us.

My desire for the text keeps driving me on, despite the painstaking work of looking up several words in each sentence and deciphering the grammar. My mind loves to read, loves the dense web of meanings that any sentence weaves. I sense the depths within the Italian sentence and feel impatient that I cannot penetrate them as effortlessly as I can an English one. I continue doggedly although the text often humiliates me, my passion winning out over my self-regard. A word like *anzi* appears over and over in an Italian text. I must look it up every time—15 or 20 times—because I can't remember what it means. *Anzi* resists memorization because it expresses a logical relationship, not anything concrete. The first time I came across *guance*, I looked it up. The second, I dimly recalled it has something to do with the face. I looked it up just to pin down which part. The third time, I paused, aware I should know this word. I reviewed the situation that the writer was describing and the surrounding words. The translation "cheeks" sprang to mind; I looked it up to confirm. Thereafter, I started to absorb the nuances of the word's usage in Italian without having to look it up. Meanwhile, I still struggle with *anzi*. I fix its meaning ("rather") in my mind, not when I have battered my memory into submission with repeated lookups, but when my soul begs for the pleasure of knowing it.

Creative reading involves sympathy between reader and text. The imagination reaches out to the words, listens to them as to a troubled friend, and assembles an idea of what is going on beneath the surface. We create a mental model of the meaning we sense there. We approximate the meaning, with all the perils of misinterpretation that this gap invites. For example, I read this line describing a character in a Spanish story:

Le cruzaba la cara una cicatriz rencorosa.[8]

At first, I treat the text as a substitution code. I look in my dictionary and translate the words one at a time: him, crossed, the, face, a, scar, angry. The crude translation gives me enough to understand this piece of the description of the character. If I wanted, I could continue reading and not lose my orientation in the story.

But that would just skate over the shallowest level of meaning. To go deeper, I rearrange the words in a way that makes sense in English: "A resentful scar cut across his face." This graceful version provides more meaning because the act of translation inveigles my imagination. I peer more deeply into the language. The words I choose reflect my instinctive interpretation of what the text conveys. *Rencorosa* can mean "angry," "rancorous," "resentful," "nasty," or some similar term, each of which connotes something different. Translation forces me to supply from my own mind the emotional background of the character in order to determine the appropriate word. I have not merely obeyed the writer; I have performed an act of creation myself.

The application of *rencorosa*, an adjective describing a human feeling, to a scar, which has no such feelings, draws my imagination still further into the text. This figure of speech collapses the distance between the scar and something or someone for which it expresses an emotion that cannot otherwise be seen. The writer does not specify which thing, though, so we must supply it for ourselves. In this way, the reader once again takes on the role of creator. Does *rencorosa* refer to the appearance of the scar? To the reaction of the man's body? To the nature of the character who is thus disfigured? To the emotion projected onto him by the narrator? By the writer? By the other characters in the story? My mind has already chosen without me realizing it. In my second version, I amended "crossed" to "cut across," and that choice implies a scar made by a blade, probably during a fight, rather than by a benign accident. Without realizing it, I have filled out the character simply by unfolding the several possibilities contained within a single word.

The connotations of a word hint at possible directions for what the text *could* mean or *could be made* to mean. Any word or expression offers a range of choices that our imagination can make without violating the rules of language. Connotations are subtle. We don't see them all. At first, our unconscious directs many of the choices we make in envisioning what the text means. We leap to one set of interpretations. However, the greater our attraction to the text, the more we linger over the words. The mind meditates upon them until further possibilities emerge. Then, we can make choices deliberately. We ask what use we can make of the text—where it can take us. Word after word resonates in our mind like images in a linguistic reverie that follow one another in not-quite-rational sequence. Sometimes, our interpretations of words connect logically, and sometimes they jump off in unexpected directions. Yet the text conveys an emotional coherence that speaks to the needs we bring to it when we read. The deep mind opens, and ideas well forth which we would never have entertained in our daylight consciousness. They are our own ideas. We feel them as well as think them, so they touch the springs of action within us. If we decide to act on them, we would not have to search for motivation.

Of course, different readers will perceive different possibilities in the same text, and I myself will perceive different possibilities there, if I come back to the text later, because I will bring a different set of needs with me. We do not have to wait, like Hammurapi's reader, for the great king to pronounce what the text means. Writers are not lawgivers. No authority coerces us into accepting that the text must mean what they say.

We pick our way through a text by conscious and unconscious decisions about what its words really mean. Naturally, a dictionary definition and usage conventions set loose conceptual limits for a word. But then each reader refers the word to some familiar realm of knowledge or experience so that it can be understood personally, not just abstractly. For example, the dictionary tells us that "fractious" means "hard to manage; unruly; rebellious; refractory" or "peevish; irritable; cross."[9] If we look up that word the first time we see it, we don't mentally substitute one of the synonyms in the definition whenever we come across it in a book—the way I do when I am starting to learn a foreign language. Rather, the synonyms point to concepts we already know. We do not need to look up "unruly" or "irritable" because we have met unruly and irritable people before, and we recognize the behavior those words refer to. All of the synonyms taken together sketch a unique range of meaning for "fractious" with many nuances. We intuit the situations that fractious describes, and we also grasp where a synonym would work better. Almost as soon as we look up a word in our native language, it leaves the realm of the substitution code and becomes a node in our mental framework. The true meaning of words and the texts they form resonates from our own lives and imaginations, not from the dictionary.

The polyvalence of language enables it to function as a transfer mechanism that can take us in a flash to far places. The reader expects one thing when he encounters a word, which then translates him to somewhere else altogether. I started by decoding *rencorosa* as a description of the man's angry-looking scar. Later, I applied it to his character and modified my translation to "resentful." Then, I wondered whether the scar makes the people who encounter him leap to conclusions about him and, therefore, reveals more about us than it does about him. The disfigured man somehow gets us to betray our own hidden *rencor*. Every word is a figure of speech. It refers to one thing on the surface but also stands for other things, always deeper and more meaningful. Words offer such a rich environment for our imagination to dwell upon that a single one can stand on its own as a text—try Googling "one word poems" to see the amount of discussion they inspire.

The dimension shifts which we have seen at the level of the individual word or sentence operate at more complex levels of language, too. Writers will often employ overt figures of speech in a passage of any length, and these rhetorical devices compare disparate things. "Shall I compare thee to a summer's day?" We tend to look at figures of speech from the writer's point of view. We wonder what the poet wished to say about his subject by making such a comparison. However, a simile or metaphor contains two terms, so the meaning can move in either direction. "Summer's day" says something about Shakespeare's beloved, but Shakespeare's beloved also says something about a summer day. Readers can choose which one to focus on, the ostensible subject of the comparison (the beloved) or the image to which it is compared (summer's day) that obtrudes unexpectedly into the encomium on her beauty. We can obey the writer and think of the subject as the main point, or we can go off on a tangent by treating the image as the main point.

Here's a famous simile from Homer's *Odyssey*. Odysseus, who is trying to return home after the Trojan War, has just suffered shipwreck and been washed ashore naked on an unfamiliar island. Exhausted, he crawls under an olive tree, heaps a pile of leaves over himself for warmth, and falls asleep. In the morning, the sound of young women playing ball wakes him. Should he lie low or approach them?

> He pushed aside the bushes, breaking off
> with his great hand a single branch of olive,
> whose leaves might shield him in his nakedness;
> so came out rustling, like a mountain lion,
> rain-drenched, wind-buffeted, but in his might at ease,
> with burning eyes—who prowls among the herds
> or flocks, or after game, his hungry belly
> taking him near stout homesteads for his prey.

(VI, 137–44)[10]

The scene is lively and moving. The comparison to the lion reveals what Odysseus did, how he appeared, how he walked, what he felt, how he affected the "flock" of young women ("he terrified them,/so that they fled, this way and that"). We think the point of the simile is to reveal something about Odysseus, the protagonist. Homer almost certainly intends this. After all, his epic tells the story of Odysseus's homecoming; he is the character whom we follow from book to book throughout the *Odyssey*.

But readers are not obligated to do what the writer wants, not even to respect the integrity of his work of art. We can pick out the bits we need and ignore the rest if we wish. We can even make the simile work in the opposite direction to the one Homer intended. For us, at this moment, understanding lions may be more important than understanding Odysseus. We flip our perspective so that the comparison with Odysseus serves to reveal something about the lion. We can sympathize with the hunger that drives a mountain lion reluctantly to attack livestock so that we no longer dismiss him as an evil predator. He must be desperate to take the risk of being hunted and killed by the farmer. The lion appears as a distinct creature, not as a mere allegory of Odysseus. We get a complete, realistic description of the lion. Some of the details match the characteristics of Odysseus ("burning eyes"). Other details describe the lion more accurately than Odysseus ("prowls among the herds," "taking him near stout homesteads"). The skill and enthusiasm with which Homer sketches the portrait suggests that the poet himself has temporarily forgotten about Odysseus in his enthusiasm for the lion.

Homer's simile works like the transfer station of a subway. We enter it going in the direction of Odysseus, and it offers us the option of switching lines and going in a completely different direction, toward lions. Likewise, we readers sense the possibilities for changing directions as we travel past the words and metaphors of any text. They constantly tug at our imagination, inviting us to stop following the writer and go off on a tangent. Each word, each syntactical unit, each figure of speech we encounter triggers the language instinct, which leads us to play with concepts to see where they might take us. The writer always wants us to keep riding on his line, but at times, we might find it more profitable to get off and go somewhere else. This conception of reading treats words as opening a gateway to further possibilities. Good readers read with their whole being. They do not drown the imagination in a stream of rational discourse, but dive and swim and allow themselves the full range of motion possible to a buoyant mind.

NOTES

1 J.N. Postgate, *Early Mesopotamia: Society and Economy at the Dawn of History* (London and New York: Routledge, 1992), p. 290. I have changed Postgate's "reveal to" to "illuminate for."

2 Anselm, *Basic Writings*, tr. S.N. Deane (La Salle, IL: Open Court Publishing Company, 1962), pp. 53–54.

3 Auerbach, p. 274.

4 Anselm, p. 3.

5 Ludwig Wittgenstein, *Philosophical Investigations*, 3rd ed., tr. G. E. M. Anscombe (New York: Macmillan Publishing Co., Inc., 1968), p. 2.

6 Dante Alighieri, *Il Convivio (The Banquet)*, tr. Richard H. Lansing (New York: Garland Publishing, Inc., 1990), p. 6.

7 Italo Calvino, *Le Città Invisibili* (Milan: Oscar Mondadori, 2009), p. 146.

8 Jorge Luis Borges, "La Forma de la Espada," in *Spanish Stories: A Dual Language Book*, ed. Angel Flores (New York: Dover Publications, Inc., 1987), p. 226.

9 *Webster's New World Dictionary of the American Language*, second college edition, ed. David B. Guralnik (New York: William Collins + World Publishing Co., Inc., 1978), p. 553.

10 Homer, *The Odyssey*, tr. Robert Fitzgerald (New York: Vintage Books, 1990), p. 103.

PART III

The functions of reading

CHAPTER 9

The world

Jules Verne demonstrates reading's most basic function in *A Journey to the Center of the Earth*: Words direct readers out into the world. Verne's novel opens as Professor Von Hardwigg—a master of the human and natural sciences, who lives in Hamburg, Germany—returns home one day after a trip to the bookstore. He had bought a volume on the history of the "Norwegian princes who reigned in Iceland," written in the twelfth century by Snorre Tarleson.[1] Von Hardwigg soon discovers that a sixteenth-century Icelandic alchemist, Arne Saknussemm, had once owned the volume. Out of the book drops a five- by three-inch slip of parchment, containing three columns of runic characters. Each column has seven rows, each row six characters. Shut inside the professor's study, Von Hardwigg and the nephew who lives with him, Henry Lawson, set about decrypting this secret message. The characters turn out to be a transliteration of a message written backwards in "dog Latin":

> Descend into the crater of Yocul of Sneffels, which the shade
> of Scartaris caresses, before the kalends of July, audacious
> traveler, and you will reach the center of the earth. I did it.
> Arne Saknussemm[2]

The message intrigues Von Hardwigg so much that he actually obeys Saknussemm's command. Dragging an unwilling Harry along with him, he travels to Iceland in June, locates the correct cone on Mt. Sneffels, and climbs deep into the earth's bowels. Thence commence the sorts of adventures that readers love Jules Verne for.

Readers instinctively respond to a challenge such as Saknussemm's. We feel the urge to adventure, the romance of it. Verne's stories work because our minds possess a perceptual map of the earth. We have absorbed innumerable details about the earth over the course of our lives, from direct experience, study, remarks by others, and so on. Our mind makes sense of this jumble of facts by assembling them into a picture. The picture offers a distorted view of the reality, with some areas appearing larger than life and very close and very detailed, while others appear smaller and sketchier and farther away. This distorted image, nevertheless, provides a framework into which we can fit new bits of knowledge. Occasionally, we revise major sections of the map after we learn more about them. Still, the basic matrix endures through all of these rounds of changes, and it fills the whole perceptual space we allot to the world. No place in the world remains an affectless blank in our minds. Even the most obscure spot evokes some image in our mind the instant we become aware of it. The mind automatically fills the blank with *something*, however erroneous. Thus, we are primed to respond with enthusiasm when we read a description of someplace we have scarcely given a thought to before. Verne's words illuminate a section of the perceptual map in our imagination with a light that looks awfully like knowledge. They elicit pleasure and curiosity. We sit up. We want to know more. If we don't go to that place ourselves, we want to hear the story of someone who has gone there so that we may experience it vicariously.

The map animates the world for us. The map means something. It does not consist of bare geometric lines and points. The coordinates 64°48′N 23°47′W do not enchant us the way the name of the place which they locate does: Sneffels. The language of a description and the perceptual map interact dynamically. They redefine one another. They belong to one another. Their mutual influence sharpens our understanding. We interpret or visualize the description through the preexisting picture of the earth we have in our mind. We already have some inkling of what Iceland is like. We can picture what a volcano looks like, guess what its internal structure might be. So the thought of someone descending into it makes conceptual sense. Verne's few hints suffice to orient us to the action of the story. At the same time, the words Verne chooses color in this part of the map with more definite feelings. On the one hand, he tells us with modern precision where the story will occur: the cone of the volcano Sneffels that the shadow of Mt. Scartaris touches in late June. The description sharpens the details in this bit of our perceptual map. On the other hand, Verne gives the landscape an archaic cast. He uses poetic language—"caresses" instead of the clinical "touches." He appeals to the moral force of the reader's character by referring to him as "audacious." He dates the time of year using the ancient Roman calendrical system ("Kalends"). This antique way of speaking warms the landscape for us. It is not a bleak desert but a welcoming environment for humanists. Verne's landscape is real to our soul. It glows with interest.

A Journey to the Center of the Earth is make-believe, but it is dangerous to be categorical. The voyage described in *Around the World in Eighty Days* also seemed improbable when Verne wrote it in 1873. In that novel, Phileas Fogg, an English gentleman, is playing whist at the Reformers' Club in London and tells his fellow card players about a newspaper article he has just read claiming that modern transportation would allow someone to circle the globe in a mere 80 days. When someone offers to wager money against it, Fogg undertakes the journey himself in order to prove that it can be done. Along the way, he has to rescue an Indian woman from suttee. He takes a tramp steamer across the Pacific. It runs out of coal and has to burn all of the wood on board, including the furniture and the boat's decking, to maintain speed. He escapes from marauding Indians in the American west. Fogg eventually returns to London, with just minutes to spare, to win the bet. Still, the reading public remained skeptical of Verne's claim. And so, in 1889, a reporter from New York set out to duplicate Fogg's route across the globe by using trains, steamships, stagecoaches, and the other modes of transport available to Verne's hero. In other words, someone set out to test a mere conceit of the imagination that Jules Verne dreamed up as the pretext for a fantasy-adventure story. Verne himself never set foot outside of France. As it turns out, not only did the reporter complete the trip; she did it in just 72 days. Her name was Nellie Bly.

Like Saknussemm's cryptogram, books inveigle us out into the world. Books have this power because sooner or later, we pose a question to ourselves about what we have read: "Is it real?" We ask this question not out of Lockean skepticism but from the soul. Some of what is in the book is not real. We know this. Still, something in the book is real, or at least our soul feels it to be real. We need to find out what it is in person so that it becomes a part of our actual lives, not just our fantasy. We glimpse in every text a possibility, and we can choose to search the world to determine whether and how it can be made real *to ourselves*. In this way, reading does not simply involve thinking about things but invites us to test our ideas against the things themselves. The test might be as quick as stepping outside at night to watch a lunar eclipse or a meteor shower that the newspaper told us about. Or we might devote our life to the trial of some religious, political, or scientific notion. Jane Goodall loved *Tarzan of the Apes* as a girl. The image of Africa in that book spurred her to go to Tanzania to study chimpanzees.

Testing a book in the world forces us to confront the chasm that separates text and thing. Every text offers a self-contained, mostly consistent environment. Books seem plausible only as long as we read them from the comfort of our study with no intention of risking ourselves on what they say. Once we decide to test a book, though, even our most basic assumptions start to fall apart. I've owned my copy of *A Journey to the Center of the Earth* since I was 11, when I bought it at Coles bookstore on Water Street in St. John's, Newfoundland. I have always understood that the name of the protagonist was Von Hardwigg. It never occurred to me to check it. The text says "Von Hardwigg." It uses the name consistently throughout. It gives me no reason to doubt the accuracy. Forty years later, I discovered that Verne had actually named the character Lidenbrock. The translator of my edition must have changed the name to Von Hardwigg for some reason. My edition (an Airmont Classic) doesn't even give the name of the translator, so I can't check his method or reputation to understand why he made this choice. If a translator could make such a fundamental alteration, what others did he make that I am still unaware of? Any changes or mistakes don't matter so long as I only want to read *A Journey to the Center of the Earth*. As soon as I want to use what I read to do something outside the book, its misalignment with the world becomes a problem.

Once we decide to test the possibilities that we glimpse in a book, the uncertainties stand out. When Harry discovers the key to Saknussemm's message, he hides the information for hours because he knows that Von Hardwigg will set off for Iceland right away to verify it. Like any sober-minded person, Harry refuses to trust his well-being to a few badly written words, which an alchemist hid inside a book 300 years before. Too many questions remain: Did they read the message accurately, considering that they had to transliterate from runic characters into the Roman alphabet, read the Latin letters backward, and translate the words from Latin into German in order to get it to come out? Could Saknussemm have been playing a trick or hallucinating? Or maybe he was simply mistaken. Suppose someone forged the message long after Saknussemm's time? Even if he really did write the message and made the trip, do the pathways he followed inside the volcano remain open? Doubts and questions multiply as soon as we start to wonder what is real in a book.

Books may be wrong, or we can easily misunderstand what we read. Some years ago, when my wife and I lived in Connecticut, a friend invited us to visit her in Durham, New Hampshire, and gave us directions. I love maps, so I seized the opportunity to get out road maps of New England. I spread them out and pored over them. My wife wondered why we couldn't just follow the directions our friend sent us. "I found a faster route," I said. On the day of our trip, we zipped through Massachusetts, avoiding Boston's rush hour traffic. We by-passed Nashua and were speeding north on a good expressway. We just needed to take the exit shown on the map, and we'd enter Durham right near our friend's house. Our friend's directions would have sent us ten miles out of the way. You can imagine my dismay when we got up to the exit indicated on the map and found that there was not an exit on the northbound side of the expressway, only on the *southbound* side. We had to drive to the next exit and double back so that we were forced to drive 20 miles out of our way to meet our friend.

Given the enormous slippage between text and world, we don't gain much if we try, like Harry, to establish the authority of the text before we go and see for ourselves. Highly proficient in Latin and Greek, Harry judges Saknussemm's message primarily by its lack of *literary* polish. It was shabby compared to the elegance of Rome's greatest poet: "[I]t seemed sacrilege to believe this gibberish to belong to the country of Virgil."[3] But no book will ever offer enough authority for us to answer all doubts and to launch ourselves securely into the world. Every text conceals gaps and fudges just as Saknussemm's did.

Moreover, Saknussemm's message requires annotations for readers to understand it fully. "Yocul" is the Icelandic word for volcano, and Sneffels (or Snaefell, meaning "snowfall") is the name of this particular volcano, Iceland's highest, which lies in the eastern part of the island. (At least, this is what my world atlas tells me if it can be trusted.) Scartaris is the name of another, perhaps fictitious peak. The Kalends is the day that starts every month in the ancient Roman calendar, which did not assign numbers to its days as we do. The Romans would specify a date by stating how many days it was before the Kalends (our 1st) or one of the two other markers in the month (Nones, roughly our 9th and Ides, roughly our 15th). In other words, we have to go outside the text in order to establish the facts it refers to. This dependence merely shifts the authority challenge to another book.

Readers must take a leap of faith when they search for the reality to which the text points. Fantasy leads to reality. Heinrich Schliemann, a rich banker from Berlin, lived about the same time as Verne. Schliemann loved Homer's two epics the *Iliad* and the *Odyssey*. Three hundred years before Herodotus, Plato, and the flowering of Athens, Homer dwelt on some poor little island in the Aegean Sea among impoverished farmers and a few pirates and traders. The nineteenth century believed in the Romantic notion that poetry is the spontaneous overflow of emotion, and the Romantics particularly valued children and primitives, who have supposedly not yet learned to mask their emotions with social conventions. Nineteenth-century experts considered Homer the finest example of a primitive genius, who just made up in his head a whole imaginary world of gods and heroes. Therefore, Schliemann seemed kooky to many scholars when his passion for Homer convinced him that the poet did not make up his material at all. Schliemann believed that Homer had described literal, historical fact in his account of the Trojan War.

Schliemann devoted his fortune to finding tangible proof of Homeric history. In 1870, he mounted an expedition to Turkey, where locals showed him an inconspicuous mound outside the tiny village of Hissarlik on the northeast Aegean coast. The classical Greeks and Romans knew it as the legendary site of Troy, but even back then, it was only a village. Nonetheless, Schliemann dug in and found that Troy really had once been a large, important city. Among many levels of occupation, he identified one that had been destroyed by a conflagration such as Homer describes and that contained a palace with rich artifacts of gold and bronze, which had once been owned, he decided, by king Priam and various other Trojans from the *Iliad*. Imagine yourself in the nineteenth century. Your education centered around learning Greek and Latin. Teachers you respected spent months or years leading you through the text of the *Iliad* and the *Odyssey*. You have always revered these books as the founding documents of Western civilization, but you think they are fictional. Now someone takes you by the hand and shows you a bronze death mask. He tells you it belongs to Priam. You are looking at the actual likeness of the king of Troy whose story you read as a student. Homer's story was real after all.

Like Schliemann, we should go where reading points us, *but we do not know what we will find when we get there.* When Schliemann arrived on site, he assumed that digging up Troy marked the end of his search. He only sought artifacts that would clinch the reality of Homer and bring him closer to those stories. Schliemann's certainty that he would find the Troy that Homer described left him unprepared to appraise what he actually did find. He proceeded without caution. On his first expedition, Schliemann engaged in indiscriminate digging, which permanently destroyed the archeological value of a large and important sector of the site. As it happens, the level Schliemann identified as Homer's Troy turns out to have flourished centuries after the traditional date of city's fall (1187 B.C.). The level that was actually occupied at the time of the supposed Trojan War (no one knows if the war ever occurred) is small—not the monumental city envisioned by Homer—and was not destroyed by fire or violence.

Schliemann eventually realized that he had uncovered something much more complex than expected—a site with a dozen or more layers of occupation covering over 1,000 years. During the remaining twenty years of his life, Schliemann developed basic techniques for scientific excavation and became a founder of classical archeology. Reading Homer literally had led Schliemann to discover a whole civilization, which had lain buried in oblivion for 3,000 years. He and other archeologists who followed him soon uncovered Bronze Age sites at places previously known only as names in Greek mythology, such as Mycenae (Agamemnon's city), Pylos (Nestor's), and Tiryns (Herakles'), which were thought to be as mythical as the Seven Cities of Gold that Coronado chased across the deserts of the American Southwest.

Places are *terra incognita* if we know them only through reading. In John Stilgoe's *Common Landscape of America*, I had once read about a small New Mexican town, Chimayo, founded in 1598 between Santa Fe and Taos.[4] Chimayo has the only town square in the United States that was laid out by Spanish settlers and never since altered. I forget whether the book showed a diagram of Chimayo's square. Certainly, Stilgoe included schematic drawings of the squares in other southwestern cities founded by the Spanish, so I could picture Chimayo's in my head. I had also previously visited the central square in Santa Fe and seen how it formed the nucleus of the modern city. When my wife and I were living in Colorado Springs, we decided we would drive down to Santa Fe again for a getaway weekend. On the way home, I persuaded my wife to take a detour to Chimayo to look for the square. We stopped at a store that sold fine handmade rugs to ask for directions. They told us what road to take. We drove about 100 yards, turned right, and passed between low, shabby houses arranged in a hollow rectangle with two openings on opposite sides for the road. The houses had been painted white, but the paint was dirty and peeling. Windows were coated with dust. The enclosure measured only about 75 by 200 feet. Overgrown grass and a few trees filled much of the space. Discarded toys and bikes lay here and there. A dirt track cut through the middle. Our car slowly rolled through and out the other side, with me still eagerly looking around for the town square, but the road seemed to be taking us into open country.

Bewildered, I turned to my wife: "Was that it?"

"I think so," she said.

The image I had formed of Chimayo from reading *Common Landscape of America* deceived me. Stilgoe had not misrepresented the square. The epic story Stilgoe told about town planning in America led me to magnify the site in my mind. I had expected a noble quadrangle, hallowed by time. Nothing about the actual place spoke of its centuries; it existed in the present just as much as we did. Historical and cultural significance did not reside innately there—that is something we import with our imagination—and as a result, for a moment, we could see Chimayo as if no one had ever thought to look at it before. In this way, the novelty of the world remains undiminished by anything we have read about it.

Like Rip Van Winkle, we sleep through the revolution. We fail to recognize new things when we meet them because our imagination struggles to escape from the biases and expectations we bring to the world. On 26 April 1336, the Italian poet Petrarch became the first person in Western history to climb a mountain just to see what was there. Mount Ventoux ("Windy Mountain") lies 60 miles due north of Marseilles, France, and 25 northeast of Avignon, where Petrarch was living in exile from his native Florence. It rises 6,263 feet above sea level and dominates the Alps in that area, between France and Italy. Petrarch recorded his ascent in a letter:

> Today, led solely by a desire to view the great height of it, I climbed the highest mountain of this region which is appropriately called Windy Mountain. The idea for this trip had been in my mind for many years. As you know, my destiny has been to live here since childhood. This mountain visible from any direction has always been in my sight. The drive to do what I did today finally overcame me, especially after having re-read some days ago in Livy's history of Rome how Philip, King of Macedonia—the one who waged the war against the Roman people—ascended Mount Hemo in Thessaly from the summit of which he believed two seas were visible, the Adriatic and the Black.[5]

Petrarch looks at Ventoux for years. Then a book spurs him to climb it. Perhaps the idea had occurred to Petrarch when he read that episode in Livy for the first time: "I've got a mountain of my own nearby that overlooks many different countries just like Hemo. I could climb it to see the kinds of things Philip must have seen." Or perhaps the idea of the ascent came of its own accord—"I wonder what it's like up there?" In any case, the idea stays in the back of his mind for years. It must have given Petrarch some image of what the top of a mountain would be like, and he decides to test the notion by going to see for himself. A second reading of Livy jolts him into action.

The episode in Livy presents more of a challenge than Arne Saknussemm's message. Saknussemm positively recommends descending into the bowels of the earth. By contrast, Livy warns against climbing mountains. Philip V ruled Macedonia (now northern Greece) for over 40 years starting about 220 B.C. He lost several campaigns to the Romans, but in 181, he considered getting revenge by invading Italy. To spy out a feasible route, he needed a high vantage point, and according to popular opinion, Mount Hemo offered a view of the Black Sea to the east, the Danube to the north, and the Alps and Adriatic to the west. Philip selected a few men and spent three days struggling up steep slopes, fighting through dense brush, and wandering in thick fog. They froze during the nights. After reaching the summit, the exhausted group took two more days to descend. "When they came down," writes Livy, "they said nothing to contradict the general notion—not because the different seas, mountains and rivers could in fact be seen from one place, but to prevent their futile expedition from providing material for mirth."[6] Philip launched no invasion. He didn't report what he saw from the top of Hemo, and Livy doesn't speculate. Or care. Probably, the view from Mount Hemo was a trivial matter for Livy. Thus, there's a hole in the record of this experience. In the thirteen centuries after Livy, most readers would have overlooked the Hemo incident entirely while the few who did think about it must have concluded that mountain climbing is arduous, dangerous, and a waste of time. It took an inquisitive mind like Petrarch's to decide to climb Ventoux to fill in what reading did not supply.

Petrarch lacked our effortless understanding of geography. Maps didn't exist, so he did not have an overhead view of the earth that showed the spatial relationships between Ventoux and the other features in that region. He would have understood point-to-point relationships between landmarks from traveling around the area. There were no photographs or even drawings of mountains, so he did not understand the sight lines from the summit. He would have seen the regular outline of Ventoux from afar, but that would not prepare him for the broken terrain of an actual mountain. And of course, no one had written a description of a mountain top before, so he did not grasp the physical experience of mountaineering. Thus, before Petrarch started the ascent, he could only imagine what Ventoux would be like based on limited knowledge. Not surprisingly, he focuses on its elevation. He says he wants to climb the mountain "to view the great height of it." In other words, he wants to look down from the top to experience the gulf between himself and the valley floor. At some point in his life, he must have stood on a rooftop or a cliff and looked down. He imagines

Ventoux as the same kind of vertiginous sensation though greatly mag-
nified. But the mountain possessed other wonders Petrarch knew he
could not imagine. To discover them, he had to go see for himself.

Petrarch's description of the summit of Mount Ventoux sounds
modern. He gives us a factual, if short, description of what he saw and
felt. The passage will seem anticlimactic to readers who have read more
spectacular accounts from modern climbers, seen sweeping, high-
resolution film of mountains, and perhaps climbed mountains themselves. But remember, this is the first account of them all:

> First of all, moved by a certain unaccustomed quality of the air
> and by the unrestricted spectacle, I stood there as in a trance.
> I looked back. Clouds were beneath me ... I then directed my
> sight toward Italy where my heart always inclines. The Alps
> themselves, frozen and snow-covered, through which [Han-
> nibal] that wild enemy of the Roman people once crossed
> and, if we believe the story, broke through the rocks with
> vinegar, seemed very close to me although separated by a
> great distance ... The boundary between Gaul and Spain, the
> Pyrenees, cannot be seen from there not because anything
> intervenes as far as I know, but because the human sight is too
> weak. However, the mountains of the province of Lyons could
> be seen very clearly to the right, and to the left the sea at Mar-
> seilles and at the distance of several days the one that beats
> upon Aigues-Mortes. The Rhone itself was beneath my eyes.[7]

Petrarch becomes entranced with the many phenomena he never imagined from down below. The summit rises more than a mile above
sea level, and the thin atmosphere would have exhausted a climber
unaccustomed to the altitude. The temperature would typically be 15–20
degrees Fahrenheit colder at the top than at the bottom. Ventoux is high
enough that cumulus clouds would sail by beneath him. He chose a fair
day for the ascent, so he commanded a panoramic view—from Italy 50
or more miles to the east, to the Alps and Lyon 90 miles to the north,
to Aigues-Mortes and Marseilles 50 or 60 miles to the southwest and
south. Petrarch finds his perspective altered so that places which would
take him several days to travel to by road seem reach-out-and-touch-it
close. He feels the exhilaration of this expansive vision. He even wishes
he could see the Pyrenees, 150 or more miles away.

Any of us today could imagine such a glorious experience. We
could easily see ourselves in Petrarch's position. We would see the
beauty of the world. We would feel awe at the vast expanse of earth

encompassed by the unbroken circle of the horizon. We would marvel at the geologic scale of time revealed in the massive rock thrust up from the earth by colliding tectonic plates. We would see the forces of erosion at work. We would notice how the species of plants and animals change as we ascend into a colder climate with less oxygen. We might meditate on the insignificance of one human life compared to the overwhelming power of nature. We would want to paint the panorama or write a poem. But all of these responses depend on a framework of science and transcendental philosophy which is less than 300 years old. Our modern conception of nature enables us to develop ideas about the meaning of the landscape and primes us for the kinds of experiences we have there. We assume such experiences are universal. They are not.

Petrarch did not possess any such conceptual framework, so his account does not imply any of the feelings about mountains that are familiar to us. Without a modern understanding of mountains, he struggles with what to make of his experience. He was an impulsive professor Von Hardwigg going up Ventoux, but once at the top, he quickly reverts to being a Harry Lawson. He turns to books to lend significance to his ascent. The sight of the Alps elicits a reference to the episode in Livy in which the Carthaginian general Hannibal surprised Rome by invading Italy through the mountains. Unlike the Philip episode, which spurred Petrarch into action, the Hannibal reference reads like the automatic response of a schoolboy asked to recall some fact about the Alps. He doesn't intend to follow in Hannibal's footsteps or to experiment with vinegar to see whether it could really split rock. When Petrarch goes on to ponder the meaning of his experience, he sounds medieval, not modern:

> While I was thus dividing my thoughts, now turning my attention to some terrestrial object that lay before me, now raising my soul, as I had done my body, to higher planes, it occurred to me to look into my copy of St. Augustine's Confessions ... I opened the compact little volume, small indeed in size, but of infinite charm, with the intention of reading whatever came to hand, for I could happen upon nothing that would be otherwise than edifying and devout. Now it chanced that the tenth book presented itself. My brother [who had come with Petrarch], waiting to hear something of St. Augustine's from my lips, stood attentively by. I call him, and God too, to witness that where I first fixed my eyes it was written: "And men go about to wonder at the heights of the mountains, and the

mighty waves of the sea, and the wide sweep of rivers, and
the circuit of the ocean, and the revolution of the stars, but
themselves they consider not." I was abashed, and, asking my
brother (who was anxious to hear more), not to annoy me, I
closed the book, angry with myself that I should still be admir-
ing earthly things who might long ago have learned from even
the pagan philosophers that nothing is wonderful but the soul,
which, when great itself, finds nothing great outside itself.[8]

Petrarch has come to the verge of modernity only to step back. He
sees the earth spread out beneath him. It makes a strong impression.
Petrarch exults. Yet he lacks the ideas to develop the experience
further. Instead, Petrarch turns away from the world and toward something familiar. He grabs onto Augustine's introspective *Confessions* for
guidance. Petrarch's purpose for reading changes. The church father
doesn't inspire Petrarch to explore a particular spot in the world as Livy
did. Augustine provides spiritual direction that applies everywhere
equally—or nowhere in particular. Augustine wants us to ignore the
earth. He wants to wrap us up in the Word of God so that we do not
extend ourselves outside of that text. Petrarch listens to the Church
Father and descends Ventoux with his eyes turned inward, which had
before looked at the earth so greedily.

Ultimately, Petrarch did not appreciate the novelty of what he had
done. He did not repeat the expedition or try to persuade others to
climb mountains. He didn't write a poem about the ascent. In fact, he
mentioned the trip to few people, perhaps because he was afraid, like
Philip, of being mocked. The seeds of something new lay dormant for
another three or four centuries until Europeans became interested in
climbing mountains for pleasure.

Petrarch's ascent did not diminish our own need to climb a mountain, nor have all the ascents made since then. The accounts that
have been written from Petrarch on may provide information about
mountains; they do not substitute for the experience or the reality of
mountains. More importantly, they do not answer any of the particular
questions each of us may have about mountains. If we do have such a
question—if our life turns on the answer—we cannot content ourselves with merely reading about mountains. Reading for information
never answers the critical questions. Instead, we must start up the slope,
where the books point us.

Few human issues are ever settled permanently. Every approach
to life is provisional although our voluminous libraries lull us into
false confidence about the extent of our knowledge. What we think

we know falls apart with surprising ease when it confronts a challenge. Even our strongest institutions rest on the unstable ground of answers that can never be known once and for all. These institutions look solid and powerful until a tremor we never imagined possible cracks foundations and topples walls. Alan Greenspan, who chaired the U.S. Federal Reserve from 1987 to 2006, advocated freeing businesses from the constraints of taxes and regulations as much as possible. This freedom would allow businesses to become more efficient and creative, with the result that the economy as a whole would grow faster. Companies driven by competition and rational self-interest would create largely self-regulating markets. Greenspan's view of free markets rested on emotional commitments. He had belonged to the circle of Ayn Rand in New York in the 1950s and early 1960s. A popular novelist and intellectual, Rand advocated a libertarian view in which heroic individuals must fight against government and bureaucratic interference to create great new businesses. Greenspan admired these ideas when he read, for instance, Rand's *Atlas Shrugged* about an entrepreneur who leads businessmen in a strike to protest taxes and regulations. He even wrote a letter to the *New York Times* praising the novel.

Greenspan applied these instincts as Federal Reserve chairman by giving financial firms and markets plenty of room to act as they wanted. During the decade of the 2000s, banks and insurance companies traded heavily in financial instruments, such as derivative contracts, credit default swaps, and mortgage-backed securities, whose risks they did not fully understand. They borrowed heavily to buy them (sometimes as much as $40 for every $1 of their own money they invested). Eventually, prices wildly exceeded the value of the underlying assets while the extensive trading left the big financial institutions beholden to each other. If one were to go bankrupt, the rest would fail in series. When the bubble burst in 2007 and 2008, the world financial system almost collapsed. Governments had to step in to save banks that had willingly entered what amounted to a financial suicide pact. The episode demonstrated that financial firms would not always act rationally as Greenspan and other free-market economists had assumed, nor could markets always correct themselves. "Those of us who have looked to the self-interest of lending institutions to protect shareholders' equity, myself included, are in a state of shocked disbelief," Greenspan confessed during a Congressional hearing.[9] It's not that Greenspan was uneducated or unsophisticated about economics. He earned a Ph.D. in that field. He served as an economic adviser in the government for many years. He had been Fed chairman for almost 20 years, during which time he had won renown for deft handling of other economic crises. The problem is that Greenspan's economic theory rested on an assumption about human nature that is false. The superstructure built on top of it collapsed as soon as reality put it to the test.

All of us stand on structures that feel solid under our feet until we step on a rotten plank which gives way under our weight. We can never be sure that the next step will support us. Our life is wholly experimental whether we admit it or not. Although Von Hardwigg seems reckless to book-bound Harry Lawson, he is the more sensible character. He knows we cannot rely on books as a store of knowledge. Instead, reading points us to what we need to test. That is its most valuable function.

NOTES

1 Jules Verne, *A Journey to the Center of the Earth* (New York: Airmont Publishing Company, Inc., 1965), p. 12.
2 Ibid., pp. 23–24.
3 Ibid, p. 17.
4 See John R. Stilgoe, *Common Landscape of America, 1585–1850* (New Haven: Yale University Press, 1981).
5 Francesco Petrarch, *Rerum Familiarium Libri I–VIII*, tr. Aldo S. Bernardo (Albany: State University of New York Press, 1975), p. 172. *Familiar Letters* IV, 1.
6 Livy, *Rome and the Mediterranean*, tr. Henry Bettenson (London: Penguin Books, 1976), p. 462. XL, 22.
7 Petrarch, pp. 175–7.
8 Petrarch, *Petrarch: The First Modern Scholar and Man of Letters*, ed. and tr. James Harvey Robinson. (New York: G.P. Putnam, 1898), pp. 316–7 cited in https://history.hanover.edu/texts/petrarch/pet17.html.
9 Edmund L. Andrews, "Greenspan Concedes Error on Regulation," in *New York Times* (23 October 2008).

CHAPTER 10

The unknown

My image of the state of human knowledge comes from Jacques Bergier's *Secret Doors of the Earth*, which I read as a teenager. The book argues that aliens from outer space left artifacts of their visits to earth in the archeological and cultural record over thousands of years. For example, Plato's legend of Atlantis recalls a great civilization built by technologically proficient visitors from another planet. The aliens have left behind an infrastructure that can connect us to the worlds where they live. The Bermuda Triangle contains such a portal, which ships and planes have stumbled into by accident and thereby vanished from this world. *Secret Doors of the Earth* fascinated me because Bergier skillfully weaves facts and wild speculation into a compelling story. The odd bits of history, myth, and archeology lend it an antiquarian richness. He presents his theories as possibilities, sources of wonder that the reader can share.

Naturally, Bergier addresses the question of why scholars and scientists have not corroborated his claims. Most writers on the occult and UFOs allege a conspiracy of silence to prevent sensational discoveries from unleashing public hysteria. Bergier offers a different explanation. He says that human knowledge is like the raisins in a steamed Christmas pudding. The pudding as a whole represents our universe. We love the raisins (what we know about the universe), but their sweetness deceives us by drawing disproportionate attention. The raisins form only a small part of the pudding, which consists mainly of thick, dark cake (what we don't know about the universe). The bits of what we do know about the universe are isolated from each other, surrounded by the unknown. We think we know a lot, but we really know little; and the little bits we know—individual research fields—don't connect with one another. Thus, Bergier's epistemology allows plenty of room for the bizarre, that is, for the imagination.

Bergier is right. Ultimately, the world is unknown. Familiar things hang suspended within the matrix of the unknown. However, we don't appreciate what the implications of this model of the universe are. We treat the unknown the same as the known. We believe that the unknown is merely the absence of knowledge, that the unknown consists of knowable things. We conceive of the unknown as a dark room full of furniture we can't see; we just have to turn on the light of our intellect to see the chairs and tables stand out in sharp outline. The unknown is as definite as the known, we believe, just deprived of light and waiting to be added to our store of knowledge.

But the unknown is *not* the same as the known. The unknown is indeterminate. Our intervention to learn it resolves certain artifacts into a fixed meaning, yet that is not the only meaning that could have emerged from the unknown. The known is simple, homogeneous, like a raisin; the unknown murky, complex, just as a Christmas pudding consists of some mixture of flour, sugar, cocoa, clove, ginger, butter, rum, eggs, and so on.

The unknown is a more accurate name for the phenomenon which the last century called the unconscious. As we saw in Chapter 3, the unconscious does not exist as a separate realm inside of us. The unconscious represents a quality that envelopes any object we encounter. Nothing comes to our attention without subjective feelings coming along, too. Nothing is purely objective in human perception. Nothing ever exists in itself; it also carries all of the potential relationships and meanings that could be teased out of it. This potentiality strikes us most vividly in the objects of a dream although objects in waking consciousness exhibit the same dream-like character to those who look for it. No firm line separates waking and dreaming, consciousness and the unconscious. They intertwine throughout every experience. The phenomenon is, therefore, much more common than the term "unconscious" suggests, which originally designated a distinct mental level rather than the ever-present quality of human experience that it really is.

The unknown hides in everything we know. Consider how to define a city. We can know it as a political entity, the "city proper." It could also be the extent of contiguous development, the metro area. It could be the buildings. It could be the utility lines. It could be the transportation networks. It could be the economic entity, determined by credit flows and other forms of exchange. It could be relationships between people. It could be the image of the city from a book or movie. It could be the area whose residents self-identify as belonging to the city. That identification will change, depending on the context. I tell people from other parts of the country that I live in Buffalo. But that would mislead fellow residents of western New York into thinking that I live in the city proper. For them, I name the particular suburb where I live. A city can be any of these things and more.

The city is undeniably real, yet it is indeterminate at the same time. When we think about a city, we usually think about one of its many aspects. We resolve the vast, indeterminate phenomenon of the city into a definite outline. As a result, the image we communicate omits the other aspects, which, nevertheless, remain implicit in it. For example, we often represent a city through one of its famous buildings: the Empire State Building, the Eiffel Tower, the Sydney Opera House. A building implies the economic history of the city—it had to make sense financially to erect that building in that place at that time. The building indicates the placement of the city's utilities and roads, the social dynamics which influence where people build, the aesthetic culture expressed in the architecture, and so on. Anytime we talk about the building, we tacitly assume all of the factors that have shaped the value it has for us today. Thus, even a place as familiar as the one we inhabit remains surrounded and shot through with the unknown because we can retain only a small number of its manifold qualities in our consciousness at a given time. The rest lie submerged in the vague field encircling the sharp, narrow idea of our city that we keep in our mind.

The unknown not only colors our perceptions; it also shapes our daily experience. When we travel through a city, we go to the places we know. We take familiar routes to get there, navigating by a few landmarks. We never travel down the vast majority of the city's streets. We never meet the vast majority of its inhabitants. We know little about what is going on in it. Still, this unknown city is just as real as the known one. The unknown city exerts secret influences that shape our life in the city we do know. We couldn't enjoy our portion of the city's amenities unless they were supported by all of the other people and relationships in the city that we will never know.

Even when we define something and make it known, the unknown lurks, waiting to reassert itself. The planks of knowledge that we tread on tend to give way just when we most need them to support our weight. Seemingly harmless assumptions lead to bizarre consequences. One of the most basic assumptions in mathematics is the Axiom of Choice, which states that one can select a specific set of points—out of the infinite set of points contained in any dimension—for use in a proof. For example, I can choose a set of points that defines a sphere with a particular center and radius. The Axiom of Choice is familiar to anyone who took high school geometry and recalls the fiat which inaugurates a problem: Assume a triangle whose hypotenuse is .... Line A-B intersects with …. Let X equal …. Using the Axiom of Choice, mathematicians have proven that a sphere can be divided into five parts and reassembled into two spheres, each of which is *equal* in volume to the first. Common sense wrestles in vain to solve that three-dimensional jigsaw puzzle. This consequence of the Axiom of Choice reminds us that we consider so many things to be solid only because they are familiar. The Axiom is really a fantasy. We treat it as true because it's useful to do so. At bottom, nothing is ever proven, so the world always remains strange, mythic.

Like geometry, each discipline requires some kind of metaphysics. It rests upon assumptions that it cannot verify within its own discipline. Businessmen believe in Adam Smith's "invisible hand," the notion that supply and demand tend toward equilibrium. This principle gives a company license to pursue its business as aggressively as it wants without worrying that doing so will destroy the market itself. Those of us in the humanities believe that studying culture makes us better people. No one has yet demonstrated it to be true. I've known a few humanists who were crummy humans. Reading Dostoevsky didn't seem to improve them. Science uncovers physical reality through repeatable experiments. We can rerun experiments under the same conditions to achieve results that do not vary over time. However, only a fraction of scientific research is ever retested because the incentives in science encourage the pursuit of original discoveries. And one third of the research findings that are retested cannot be replicated. Even the most reliable truth claims rest upon untestable assumptions. We believe that physical laws remain constant in time and space although we have not proved that they do. We trust this hypothesis because it is useful and has not yet been falsified although some physicists speculate that different physical laws do apply elsewhere in the universe.

The fundamental assumptions upon which a discipline is built generally don't cause problems as long as we stay within that field. For this reason, we give most of our attention and resources to problems that can be addressed within the limits of individual academic disciplines—medicine, aerospace, economics, history, anthropology, astrophysics, and so on. Within these limits, we have developed an impressive amount of knowledge. Thus, we can remove tumors from almost anywhere in the body, send communication satellites into orbit, understand the economics of bubbles and crashes, analyze the causes of the Civil War, study indigenous cultures in the Amazon, measure the age of the universe, and so on.

Our assumptions fail when we try to tackle problems outside of a particular discipline, and indeed, the toughest problems we face span areas of knowledge. For this reason, we struggle to

- Determine when the expense, suffering, and complications of surgery outweigh the benefits to patients
- Send effective messages via those satellites
- Keep bubbles from forming in the first place
- Use our historical knowledge to prevent wars or heal the divisions caused by war
- Preserve the rain forest where the Amazonian Indians live
- Explain what the universe means.

These problems cross the boundaries of specialized knowledge—medicine and philosophy; communications and language; economics and politics; history, diplomacy, and politics; anthropology, environmentalism, and law; and astrophysics and the humanities. We cannot solve these complex problems simply by adding together the relevant specializations because the heart of the problem lies somewhere in between them, in the unknown. We cannot arrive at a solution unless we deal with the indeterminate messiness of the unknown.

We commit our greatest blunders when we treat the unknown the same as the known and misapply our knowledge. Ezra Pound reinvigorated the humanistic tradition with energy and imagination in the early twentieth century. He revolutionized poetry with his ideogrammic method in which he juxtaposed blocks of text on disparate subjects, often quoted from other writers, to spark new insights in the reader. His masterpiece, *The Cantos*, ranks with the *Iliad* and the *Divine Comedy* as epics that define a cultural age. Pound learned to read in nine languages. He read voraciously about art, music, literature, philosophy, history, economics, politics, and other subjects. Young writers would come to visit Pound to study at what they dubbed the Ezuversity.

Pound wanted to restore the values of the Renaissance, when political leaders and artists alike devoted themselves to humanistic ideals. That commitment led him to despise capitalism, which he viewed as responsible for evils such as the international arms race and cultural decay. Pound was convinced that "the world Jewish conspiracy" of capitalists threatened all that was good. Mass production, he believed, makes things "cheap" in both senses and preempts demand for the high-quality productions of artist and craftsman. Pound, therefore, advocated the ideas of a reactionary Canadian political party of the 1930s, Social Credit. He argued that governments should replace money with scrip, which would come with an expiration date. Scrip would retain its value for only a few weeks and then become worthless. People could use it to buy what they needed to live and would naturally purchase the best quality goods they could find, rather than buying cheap things and saving the remainder of their earnings as they can with money. Thus, no one could hoard scrip and over time accumulate economic power.

For Pound, interpreting the economy posed no more risk than interpreting Provençal poetry. He treated both as moral exercises. The reality of people's jobs, income, and lives did not penetrate his Olympian consciousness. Scrip would have eliminated all the benefits of a modern economy—saving for education or a house, raising capital for new factories and hiring workers, giving entrepreneurs an incentive to bring inventions to market, and so on—and plunged millions into poverty.

Pound clung to his moralistic view of the world throughout the 1930s and 1940s. A long-time resident of Italy, Pound supported Benito Mussolini, Italy's fascist dictator. For *The Cantos*, Pound wrote two laudatory poems in Italian during World War II especially for Mussolini (Cantos 72 and 73). The United States suffered over 100,000 casualties fighting in Italy. Therefore, Pound's publisher understandably did not want to print the two poems—editions of *The Cantos* omitted them. They did not appear till an academic journal published them four decades later. During the war, Pound readily agreed to broadcast on behalf of Mussolini to the United States and its troops in Europe. On the radio, Pound ranted about how President Franklin Delano Roosevelt and "the Jews" were destroying Europe. Arthur Miller, who heard the original broadcasts, thought Pound should have been shot as a traitor. When U.S. forces captured the province in which Pound lived, the local Italians pointed him out. Pound was arrested, held for a time at a U.S. Army prisoner of war camp in Pisa, and then sent back to Washington, D.C., to stand trial. The U.S. government did plan to try Pound for treason, but literary figures intervened, notably Pound's friend T.S. Eliot. They argued that Pound was a literary giant and, anyway, was only a harmless poet. Pound was declared "insane" and sent to St. Elizabeth's mental hospital in Washington, where he received guests and continued to write. He was released in 1958 and allowed to return to Italy.

Up to this point in his career, Pound never wavered in his views, never stopped expressing his opinions loudly (though he muted his voice when he thought government prosecutors were listening). Could Pound have been unmoved by revelations about the Holocaust after the war? Did he feel some remorse when he found out that Mussolini had a concentration camp a few miles from Pound's house in Rapallo where he collected Italian Jews for shipment to Nazi death camps like Auschwitz? Indeed, when Pound returned to Italy at age 73, he suddenly began to doubt the ideas he had developed over the previous 50 years: "I have come upon a great uncertainty," he said, "too late in life for it to do me any good." The Pound who had expressed himself vociferously up to this point now fell silent—literally. At one point, he would communicate with people only by blinking his eyes, once for "yes," twice for "no." Upon reflection, what did Pound conclude about his relationship with fascism? "I only admired the fascist monetary system. I didn't want to burn children." He makes it sound like an innocent mistake.

That is a lame explanation, given the bleak contrast between Pound's reverence for humanistic values and the human catastrophe caused by the fascist regime he worked for. All of Pound's reading did not save him. He counted too much on the positive accumulation of learning and ignored the value of uncertainty. A greater respect for the unknown—negative capability, Keats would say—might have kept him from being swallowed up by the darkness.

Innocence is dangerous, the innocence that knows only what it knows. Pound thought he had found the eternal principles of the good life. He referred to great poetry as "news that stays news"; it retains its value for all time and in all places. One needs this level of conviction about goodness to embrace evil with open eyes. The innocent live in the daylight of consciousness. They do not allow their heroic intellect to fall asleep. To the innocent, dreams and nightmares are merely weird distortions of the waking world, not secret doors to other possibilities.

The end of Plato's *Symposium* illustrates the errors that wakeful intellects like Pound's make. I always smile when I read it. The dialogue records what Aristodemus, a guest, saw and heard at a party in honor of Agathon, who had just won first prize in the annual competition for tragic playwrights at Athens' Great Dionysia festival. (He must have beat out the likes of Sophocles and Euripides.) Aristophanes, the great writer of comedies, was there and, of course, Socrates. It's the early morning hours, and everybody has already been drinking and talking for a long time:

> Aristodemus reported that … [h]e himself fell asleep and slept for some time, as the nights were long at that time of year. Towards daybreak, when the cocks were already crowing, he woke up, and found that the rest of the party had either fallen asleep or gone away, and that the only people still awake were Agathon and Aristophanes and Socrates. They were drinking from a large cup which they passed round from left to right, and Socrates was holding forth to the others. Aristodemus did not remember most of what passed … but the main point was that Socrates was compelling them to admit that the man who knew how to write a comedy could also write a tragedy, and that a skillful tragic writer was capable of being also a comic writer. They were giving way to his arguments, which they

> didn't follow very well, and nodding. Aristophanes fell asleep
> first, and when it was fully light Agathon followed him.
>   Then Socrates, having put both his interlocutors to sleep,
> got up and went away ... He went to the Lyceum and washed,
> and spent the day as he would any other, and finally towards
> evening he went home to bed.[1]

It's a big joke on Socrates, revered for twenty-four centuries as the Wisest Man because of his modesty: he alone admitted that he knew little. Here, though, Socrates presumes to teach two great dramatists about their art, and he wins the argument not because he's smarter but because he's got more stamina. He bullies them. He keeps talking longer than everyone else. He stays awake while they fall asleep.

This unflattering view of Socrates highlights the blindness of the intellect. Plato draws a contrast between Socrates' apparent strength and other people's apparent weakness. The Great Dionysia was held around the spring equinox, when day and night are in balance. But Aristodemus insists that "the nights were long at that time of year" as if to paint a darker background against which Socrates' wakefulness can stand out more. The Great Dionysia honored Dionysos, of course, who was the god of wine, revelry, and disorder—the loosening of conventional restrictions on behavior. We saw these attributes of Dionysos in Euripides' *The Bacchae*, discussed in Chapter 5. Appropriately to the occasion, the party guests pass around a large wine cup. The alcohol works its characteristic effect as, one by one, people fall asleep. They have succumbed to the influence of Dionysos. Their slumber acknowledges his divinity.

However, the wine and the party which have continued throughout the night and into full morning have not affected Socrates at all. Not only does he not fall asleep; he spends the day after the party going about his business as if it were any ordinary day. Socrates is immune to the influence of Dionysos. After he leaves the party, he goes to work out at the Lyceum, a gymnasium which was situated at the temple of Apollo Lyceus at Athens. Apollo is the god of the sun and by extension the sunshine of the intellect, of rules, sobriety, and physical culture. A healthy mind in a healthy body. Thus, Apollo governs instincts opposed to those of Dionysos. Both the physical stamina and the intellectual stamina that Socrates uses to win the argument at the party come from his cultivation of Apollo.

Socrates hasn't really won anything, though, in the debate at the after party. He was "compelling [Agathon and Aristophanes] to admit" something against their will. "They were giving way to his arguments, which they didn't follow very well ..." He has not genuinely persuaded them and for good reason. In the end, Socrates' deepest thoughts about drama cannot turn Agathon into a good comic writer and Aristophanes into a good tragic writer. No amount of logic and talking can change someone's inborn talent. Socrates has won an intellectual game. He has not altered the world. The content of our mind matters, but the context in which we employ it matters more. By itself, intellectual training, including the Socratic method, is never adequate. To create something of value with our intellect, we have to use it in a messy world inhabited by real people. We have to go where they are, not keep to the realm of pure thought. For all his intellectual strength, Socrates cannot force people to stay with him on that level. When he confronts Agathon and Aristophanes with an argument which experience shows to be false yet whose logic they cannot refute, they fall asleep. They drift off into a different kind of consciousness, joining their fellow party guests in the dream world where minds find refreshment. Meanwhile, Socrates remains trapped within his sunny consciousness. He goes off by himself and spends the day seemingly alone.

The limitations of consciousness furnish the theme of a key episode in the epic of Gilgamesh. Gilgamesh is the hero of an old Mesopotamian story cycle. The most complete version we have was composed around 1200 B.C., but it is based on Sumerian stories that are at least 1,000 years older than that. In the epic, after numerous adventures together, Gilgamesh's best friend dies. The hero suffers what we would call an existential crisis and travels to the distant land of Dilmun (today's Bahrain) in search of immortality. In Dilmun lives Utnapishtim, who knows how to contact the gods, who can grant immortality. The gods gave this island paradise to Utnapishtim as a reward because he saved the human race from extinction in a universal flood. (The authors of *Genesis* modeled Noah after him.) Utnapishtim says that he is willing to assemble the gods for Gilgamesh, but Gilgamesh must first pass a test: "only prevail against sleep for six days and seven nights."[2] If Gilgamesh were capable of staying awake this long, he wouldn't need to seek immortality. He would already be a god because the gods alone remain perpetually awake.

Utnapishtim plays this trick to demonstrate Gilgamesh's human frailty. We humans seldom remain awake longer than 20 hours at a stretch, and no mere effort of will can prolong consciousness for more than a few hours beyond the time allotted for it in our circadian rhythms. So it was with Gilgamesh:

> But while Gilgamesh sat there resting on his haunches, a mist of sleep like soft wool teased from the fleece drifted over him, and Utnapishtim said to his wife, "Look at him now, the strong man who would have everlasting life ..."

The wife wants to shake Gilgamesh awake, tell him he failed, and send him home. Utnapishtim, though, knows that Gilgamesh's very lack of consciousness means that, even if wakened, he would not realize his own weakness. Instead, Utnapishtim asks his wife to bake a loaf of bread for each day that Gilgamesh sleeps:

> So she baked loaves of bread, each day one loaf, and put it beside his head, and she marked on the wall the days that he slept; and there came a day when the first loaf was hard, the second loaf was like leather, the third was soggy, the crust of the fourth had mold, the fifth was mildewed, the sixth was fresh, and the seventh was still on the embers. Then Utnapishtim touched him and he woke. Gilgamesh said to Utnapishtim the Faraway, "I hardly slept when you touched and roused me." But Utnapishtim said, "Count these loaves and learn how many days you slept ..."[3]

Far from demonstrating the stamina of a god, Gilgamesh snoozes the whole time! Gilgamesh's nap symbolizes the mental state in which we normally live. Mundane tasks occupy most of our waking moments. When we get up in the morning, we plunge into our daily routine of work or school. On weekends, we do chores or entertain ourselves. Only in brief moments do we attain the clarity and attention with which we can bring a new idea into the world. From the standpoint of godlike creativity, then, we spend almost all of our lives unconscious.

This awareness changes our conception of knowledge. Like Pound, we tend to think of knowledge as "news that stays news." A piece of knowledge always remains the same. Its permanence allows us to defeat time. In fact, we are confusing knowledge with information or principles. Knowledge is much more fleeting. It is a brief intersection between the known and the unknown. It is like the aroma of the bread that Utnapishtim's wife baked. When fresh, bread exhales a rich smell and has a flavor far more delicious than the sum of the butter, flour, and yeast that went into it. After a day, however, this bouquet deserts the hardened loaf. The bread looks the same—we can still tear it apart, chew it, fill our belly with it—but it no longer pleases as before. If we don't want to sustain our minds on moldy bread, we must bake every day. Thus, knowledge becomes the daily practice of finding a humble, new idea to illuminate a small bit of the unknown which envelopes us.

The unknown flows into the gaps in the facts we possess and the methods we use—all of the disconnections, divergences, errors, deceit, and overconfidence to which rational minds fall prey. Recall the aphorism of Heraclitus, quoted by James Hillman in Chapter 3: "The real constitution of each thing is accustomed to hide itself ..." In other words, we are compelled to go looking if we want to understand something in any meaningful way. Meaning is never self-evident. It is generated by the very act of searching for it. However, we cannot derive meaning from the unknown unless we use different means to explore it than ones we apply to the known world. Since meaning consists of fleeting insight into the hitherto unknown connections between things, subtleties matter rather than logic, and reading is a better instrument for discerning them.

Subtleties are easy to dismiss or overlook. It took more than a century for economists to arrive at a theory of value that businessmen could use to set prices systematically rather than intuitively. Alfred Marshall formulated the theory of marginal utility in 1890: a commodity's price is determined by the last, or marginal, unit that consumers are willing to pay for. The price of a can of soup reflects how much shoppers want it, relative to all of the other things they could spend their money on. Adam Smith, Karl Marx, and other great economists before Marshall failed to arrive at this solution because they recycled the faulty assumptions and sloppy expressions of prior writers. They did not read with enough sensitivity.

For a long time, people imagined that economic value was a kind of substance that was inherent in a commodity or added during production. French *philosophe* François Quesnay proposed in 1760 that economic value was an "energy" drawn from the soil by farmers and miners. No one else created value; people merely transferred the original energy from hand to hand when they exchanged goods. In 1776, Adam Smith suggested that the value of a commodity was its cost of production, especially labor costs. The process used to make something fixed economic value in it.

In 1803, Jean-Baptiste Say stated,

> It is universally true, that, when men attribute value to any thing, it is in consideration of its useful properties: What is good for nothing they set no price upon ... And I will go on to say, that, to create objects which have any kind of utility, is to create wealth; for the utility of things is the ground-work of their value, and their value constitutes wealth.[4]

Here, 87 years before Marshall, the term "utility," the lynchpin of his theory, entered economists' vocabulary. For Say, however, utility meant an objective property fixed in a commodity by labor—the hardness of iron, say—not the consumer's subjective feeling that the commodity will fill one of his needs.

The theory of marginal utility might have arisen sooner, except that another great economist confused things. In 1817, David Ricardo wrote, "Possessing utility, commodities derive their exchangeable value from two sources: from their scarcity, and from the quantity of labor required to obtain them."[5] Although Ricardo understood how demand controls the market—he was the best securities trader in London— he couldn't bring himself to abandon Smith's notion that labor puts value into a product. However, Ricardo almost casually turned the perspective around from the producer's labor to the consumer's, without pursuing the implications of this point further.

In 1848, John Stuart Mill accepted Smith's labor theory but also extended Say's idea about utility by distinguishing three kinds: "utilities fixed and embodied in outward objects," "utilities fixed and embodied in human beings" as skills (such as those of a doctor or a welder), and utilities "consisting in a mere service rendered, a pleasure given, an inconvenience or a pain averted."[6] With his first and third items, Mill seems to draw a distinction between the objective and subjective properties of a commodity, between what a commodity is and what it means for the consumer.

However, when Marx published *Capital* in 1867, he cited Ricardo's authority to assert once more that labor is the essence of value, yet unlike Ricardo, Marx emphasized production over consumption or demand. Thus, not until very late in the nineteenth century did Alfred Marshall hammer out a complete theory of value. His work appeared 130 years after the first attempt to address the problem.

Marshall did not arrive at the theory of marginal utility by employing fancier math or more sophisticated experiments than economists used before him. Rather, he went back to just plain reading in sorting through the mountain of ideas and errors accumulated by the authors of classical economics. In his *Principles of Economics*, Marshall repeatedly shows that he defined his own views through a close reading of his predecessors' work. He appreciated nuances in the wording of key ideas. At one point, for example, Marshall interrupted his main discussion to insert an eight-page "Note on Ricardo's Theory of Value." He believed that others had misconstrued what Ricardo was trying to say:

> Ricardo's theory of cost of production in relation to value
> [which I quoted above] occupies so important a place in the
> history of economics that any misunderstanding as to its real

character must necessarily be mischievous; and unfortunately
it is so expressed as almost to invite misunderstanding.[7]

Marshall then proceeds to analyze Ricardo's 23-word formula phrase by phrase.

Marshall's treatment of Ricardo illustrates two points. First, Marshall recurred to the ancient, creative way of reading. A critical reader would have looked at the passage from Ricardo and parsed its words in order to find out what Ricardo really meant. We do so because we want to make our views seem the inevitable consequence of established knowledge rather than unfounded speculation. This impulse is based on two assumptions: the earlier writer contains the essential nugget of truth that will solve our problem, and we can find it if we look closely enough. We moderns have a tendency to overdetermine the meaning of what we read out an abundance of respect for the authors. More likely, the authorities we revere share our fallibility. If Ricardo's formulation is unclear, it's because his thinking was unclear, not that his thinking was sharp but we lack the perspicacity to see it. Marshall was really just using Ricardo's words as a medium through which to glimpse possibilities that Ricardo never thought of. Like ancient readers, Marshall accorded reality to Ricardo's words rather than to any external truth they supposedly pointed at.

The second point illustrated by the Marshall example is that the reader should *approach* the purported meaning of the text, but not put a finger precisely on it even if that were possible. Marshall treats the text as a portal to the unknown, not as a repository of definite knowledge. Ricardo uses a number of terms that prove important for Marshall, who, nevertheless, understands them in quite a different way than Ricardo does or takes them much further than Ricardo did. As in Say, Ricardo's "utility" refers to objective properties (the hardness of iron), whereas Marshall gives it a subjective meaning—commodities have utility *for the consumer*. Ricardo talks about the absolute "scarcity" of a commodity, but something may be scarce without possessing any value because nobody wants it. Marshall translates this idea into relative scarcity, the ratio of demand to supply. A commodity that is abundant in absolute terms (such as gold) may still be relatively scarce because of high demand for it. Ricardo talks about "exchangeable" value, which Marshall develops into the full-blown idea that a commodity has no inherent value but only what the consumer is willing to pay for it. (Homeowners under water with their mortgage will understand what I mean all too well.) Smith and Marx talked about value in relation to the labor used to produce a commodity, but Marshall amplifies Ricardo's hint that what counts is the "labor required to obtain" the commodity. The consumer works to obtain money with which to buy a commodity. The amount of money he has factors into his calculation about whether the commodity is worth buying at a given price. In sum, Marshall the reader has slightly altered the tenor of key terms in Ricardo to produce a new, more powerful understanding of economic value.

The creative reading that Marshall demonstrates here springs from tiny sparks of intuition and experience generated by the friction of a text passing through an attentive mind. The reader must respond to these little insights immediately or lose them like a name on the tip of our tongue that slips from our mental grasp. If the reader waits too long, he can at best render a leaden approximation that misses the essential connection. One spring day, the sun shining, the ground thawing, I came up with a theory of image for Baldassare Castiglione's *The Courtier* on my walk home from school. I saw why image forms the book's central point. I saw it so clearly that I experienced that sweet pleasure of the intellect equivalent to being in the zone in sports. I decided I would write a paper about my idea. The insight seemed so vivid I didn't bother to jot down notes about it. By the next day when I sat down to start my essay, I had forgotten my idea. That is, I still had in mind the scene in *The Courtier* I was thinking about when the idea occurred to me. I recall that Castiglione's characters are in a room, the clouds suddenly part, and sunlight comes through a stained-glass window. But the exact significance had fled out of my head beyond retrieval. I didn't bother trying to write the essay.

A good reader knows enough to foster such insights like sparks in tinder. At first, the insight exists as a mere wisp of feeling deep in our mind. We struggle to prolong it and then to amplify the feeling enough to appraise it. We turn it this way and that in our mind to get a better view. We look at it edge on, like a coin on a table top that seems barely visible, until we flip it up to reveal one of its faces, stamped with an eloquent image and a value. We scarcely yet know what the idea is. We have not grasped its essence or followed out its implications. In that moment, something has come to the threshold of knowledge without yet losing the energy and sense of possibility that generated it. It's the closest we can ever come to seeing the unknown, which surrounds us and qualifies all of our lives.

NOTES

1 Plato, *The Symposium*, tr. Walter Hamilton (New York: Penguin Books, 1951), pp. 113–14.
2 *The Epic of Gilgamesh*, tr. N.K. Sandars (New York: Penguin Books, 1972), p. 114.
3 Ibid., p. 114f.
4 Jean-Baptiste Say, *A Treatise on Political Economy; or The Production, Distribution and Consumption of Wealth*, tr. C. R. Prinsep (Philadelphia: John Grigg, 1830), p. 2.
5 David Ricardo, *The Principles of Political Economy and Taxation* (London: J. M. Dent & Sons Ltd., 1992), p. 5.
6 John Stuart Mill, *Principles of Political Economy with Some of Their Applications to Social Philosophy*, ed. J. M. Robson, *Collected Works*, vol. 2 (Toronto: University of Toronto Press, 1965), pp. 46–47.
7 Alfred Marshall, *Principles of Economics*, 2nd ed, vol. 1 (London and New York: Macmillan and Co., 1891), p. 538.

CHAPTER 11

Reading in the digital age

A crisis has enveloped reading such as it has never seen before. The proportion of college diplomas awarded in the humanities has plummeted to the lowest level on record. Many students don't see a bright future for themselves if they hold a humanities degree. Data and analytics promise more definitive answers to the kinds of issues that only the erudite used to discuss with authority—love, politics, the good life, and so on. Some announce the death of reading. For example, David Trend proclaims an end to literacy based on books in *The End of Reading: From Gutenberg to "Grand Theft Auto."* Others plead for the value of reading as if to commute a capital sentence. Psychology studies attest that reading literature increases empathy. Apparently, literature must now rely on statistical surveys to prove its worth, reading having been judged incompetent to testify on its own behalf.

But outside the courtroom, the case looks quite different. Reading remains as popular as ever. Book sales in the United States continue near all-time highs, with 2.7 billion volumes sold in 2017. Independent booksellers are defying the onslaught of big online merchants. The United States has over 100,000 book clubs. Formal efforts such as The Reader project in the United Kingdom bring people together around shared texts. When CEOs are asked what skills their workforces will need in the future, their lists read like a mission statement for the humanities: creativity, critical thinking, cultural awareness, mental agility, communication, empathy, and so on.

In fact, reading is not failing; rather, traditional cultural institutions built around books are failing. The context in which these institutions developed has changed dramatically. Some of the assumptions upon which they were founded no longer hold true. In particular, the humanities traditionally revolved around scarcity or selectivity. Only certain books were available, and only certain people had the leisure to read them; someone needed to select the best books and teach people how to read them the right way. These conditions held true until well into the twentieth century but then rapidly disappeared.

Geoffrey Chaucer boasted of owning 60 books in 1400. In 1907, Ezra Pound found that the Wabash College library in Indiana held 40,000 volumes—the total knowledge available to someone in that location. Access to books had increased on the order of 1,000 times in 500 years. Even so, each book was precious, not something to take for granted. Scarcity drove people's behavior. A professor of mine once took leave to teach American literature in southern Africa. On the first day of class, he set a box of books he had brought in front of the class and invited students to borrow any volumes they might need. When he turned around, the box was empty, such was the unmet demand for books. Anyone who has used Amazon struggles to comprehend this hunger. Today, someone with an Internet connection can access 30–40 million books. In the last century, therefore, access to books has increased again on the order of 1,000 times. Google estimates that the total number of books that have ever been written in the history of the world is 130 million. We are approaching universal access to books. From here on, access will continue to increase although the exponential gains of the past are no longer possible.

The availability of books alters their value and that of their readers and writers. The importance of the writer diminishes as access increases. If our universe of books consists of a few hundred or a few thousand volumes, the universe of ideas to which we are exposed will be similarly small. Any new book that a writer adds to this store changes the way we think about the world. Thus, the writer matters more than the reader. When we have instant access to tens of millions of volumes, however, virtually anything we need is already available. New authors and new books do not contribute as much value. Instead, we readers create more value by carefully choosing books to read and then creating something from our experience of them.

A Dante or a Milton had read every important book available in his world. Even into the twentieth century, people could still plausibly claim as much for an Ezra Pound or a Charles Olson. We cannot say the same now that we are awash in an ocean of books. Even if we could identify the best 0.1% of them, there would still be many times more books than the most dedicated reader could get through in a lifetime. No one can speak with as much cultural authority as those poets once did.

When one can afford to keep only hundreds or thousands of volumes, someone has to choose the best ones. The traditional gatekeepers, including publishers, editors, librarians, teachers, and critics, cannot digest millions of books in order to find the most valuable ones. Any recommendations necessarily reflect the narrow purview of the gatekeeper. For this reason, people increasingly find institutions for filtering books of limited value to their lives. Readers know when institutions do not speak to them, and they soon find alternative sources that do. New forms of reading are starting to emerge that revolve around the reader. Today's readers find their own way. Readers curate texts for themselves and share their findings with their social networks. They read and discuss books as part of a community, either in person or via social media. These peer-to-peer relationships increasingly shape opinion. In this way, readers have started to exercise more cultural power than authors do by writing something new.

Old habits of thought about reading persist and impede the new ways of reading that continue to develop. Book clubs often select works from the Western literary canon as defined in the mid-twentieth-century because that was the last cultural consensus around reading. We will have to jettison this most sacred filter of literary culture in order to clear the way for new forms of reading that better suit the open-ended conditions of a digital world.

The idea of a canon encodes restrictive assumptions about reading. The Middle Ages distinguished a set of *auctores*, or authors whose work exemplified principally grammatical correctness. The *auctores* were the textbooks one used in learning to read and write Latin. During the Renaissance, the canon of *auctores* expanded into our notion of the "classics" in the wider sense, that is, works exemplifying the ideal in all respects: morally, intellectually, and artistically as well as grammatically. The canon collected and displayed all the virtues to which European culture aspired, and the works of the canonical authors became the standard against which people judged themselves.

This notion of the classics was stamped onto English literature in the middle of the nineteenth century by Matthew Arnold, a classically trained poet, Oxford professor, and inspector of schools for the British government. The terrible effects that the Industrial Revolution had on the working class appalled Arnold. He saw it as the cause of poverty, drunkenness, and violence. Arnold wanted to rescue workers from their "immoral" lives by educating them in what he felt were the proper values, and he thought that, since they could not be educated to read the Greek and Latin classics, they could learn these values best through reading English literature.[1] Arnold started to make a literary canon out of books written in English to parallel the canon of ancient texts. The works of Shakespeare and Milton transformed from being simply enjoyable books to read into becoming models for people to admire and learn from. Thus, Arnold gave literature a quasi-religious function by asking it to reform the brutality of the world. He broached this idea in 1867 in *Culture and Anarchy*: "Now, then, is the moment for culture to be of service, culture which believes in making reason and the will of God prevail, believes in perfection ..."[2]

Arnold's faith in the power of literature to help reform industrial society shows a misunderstanding of the new economic realities. As the slave trade taught the nineteenth century and the drug trade teaches us today, the law of supply and demand does not stop working when it transgresses morality. But in his search for perfection Arnold rejected the real world quite consciously. He separated culture from "curiosity," that is,

> the scientific passion, the sheer desire to see things as they are ... Culture is then properly described not as having its origin in curiosity, but as having its origin in the love of perfection; it is *a study of perfection*.[3]

And the function of literature, according to Arnold, is that it articulates the ideals toward which society strives.

Arnold's idealism contains a familiar contradiction. On the one hand, he wants literature to influence the world: literature will make society better. On the other hand, literature can point us toward perfection only by standing apart from the daily, often sordid realities of life. Thus, Arnold's notion of literature, which we have inherited, often frustrates us. We think of literature as IMPORTANT, yet it deliberately keeps its relationship to our life vague. It refuses to identify a specific place where we can make use of it.

Years ago, I went to the dentist for a checkup. I sat down in the examining room, and the hygienist clipped a napkin under my chin and lowered the chair back till I was looking up at the ceiling. Very friendly, she asked me what I did for a living. I told her I taught English. She said that she had always wanted to read the classics to improve herself. What were the top ten books? I replied that such a list could only be arbitrary and that she should just read whatever she liked best. She pressed me to name titles. I resisted. After some back-and-forth, she grew exasperated. She stopped her preparations for the exam, looked straight down at me and demanded I give her at least one title. I couldn't very well tick her off since she was about to run a steel scaler under my gums. For some reason, though, my mind felt dry. I couldn't think of any inspired suggestion, so I blurted out a book that I thought my professors would have said any American should read: *The Scarlet Letter*. By chance, I never went back to that dentist, so I don't know whether the hygienist ended up reading Nathaniel Hawthorne's novel or not. I hope she did and enjoyed it. If she's like most people, though, she'll spend the rest of her life feeling slightly guilty that she hasn't read it because she knows it would be "good" for her. Or perhaps she gritted her teeth and slogged through to the book's end. I once pushed through Thomas Carlyle's translation of Goethe's *Wilhelm Meister's Apprenticeship*, the most boring book I've ever read, so I know what it's like. Either forced reading or not reading at all is a likely outcome when people think about reading like taking vitamins rather than as a matter of appetite and necessity like eating.

The hygienist's insistence on getting a list of classics to read demonstrates how pervasive the notion of the literary canon has become. Almost everybody thinks about "literature" as a set of books that improve the people who read them. The literary canon inculcates self-knowledge, morality, worldliness, and critical thinking. The books included in the canon are the old books, ones that the most cultured readers have admired for generations. Some countries built official institutions around the canon, such as the *Académie Française* and the *Real Academia Española*. In the United States, the institutions are informal. The Great Books educational curricula began in the early twentieth century—for example, the Harvard Classics. The Great Books aimed to illustrate a coherent set of ideas which have developed over time to shape the world we live in today. Students and others could read the Great Books to learn the Western tradition and become better people. The Great Books offered both grandeur and convenience. One would need to read only, say, 100 books to join the ranks of the educated. The Great Books also conveyed a sense of obligation since they set a minimum standard of knowledge for citizens.

This is the image of literature that my dental hygienist had in mind. She felt an obligation to read literature but never a definite impulse or need to do so, nothing to convert inclination into action. She thought she lacked the willpower and wished she weren't so lazy. Instead, the very idea of a literary canon or a Western tradition creates the circumstances for these all-too-common failures. Literature sits apart from and above the world. A few people discover a perverse desire to read it. Otherwise, no natural connection links literature to the common joys and challenges of life.

The literary canon lies at the center of today's debate between traditionalists and multiculturalists to determine the proper cultural role of reading. In the United States, the so-called culture wars erupted around 1990 when liberals and conservatives dueled over educational philosophy and classroom curricula. Conservatives charged liberals with promoting multiculturalism at the expense of what they see as the mainline tradition "that unites, even defines America."[4] Traditionalists want people to read literature to learn the core values of Western culture; they think literature ought to serve a *unifying* function. But multiculturalists argue that the conservative view is too narrow and that the literary canon should be enlarged to give people an appreciation of cultural *diversity* in America and throughout the world. Many critics today talk about how texts written by people in marginalized groups, such as women, blacks, and gays, "subvert" prevailing cultural norms—as though subversion in itself is valuable. But the multicultural approach still conserves the idea of a canon, if only by contradiction.

In the future, the emphasis will shift from which books we ought to read to what we can create from whatever we do read. This shift will better align reading to an open world. Within the last generation or two, the world has become more accessible, closer to us—dangerously so at times. It has also become more diverse. Although Western literature will remain important, our interest in other cultural spheres will grow. Immigration from there will continue, and immigrants will bring with them an interest in their roots. Globalization will put workers and students in daily contact with people from around the world. Therefore, it will pay us to learn more about the long, rich cultural traditions of China, India, and the Arab world. We will benefit from comparing the new-world experiences of Latin America, and the postcolonial experiences of Africa and Southeast Asia to our own experiences. We will also feel the weight of Japan, Russia, and many other countries that continue to build on strong cultural foundations. We cannot construct a literary canon that could represent the moral and intellectual values of this vast globe. The scale of the world has far outgrown the snug boundaries of a canon. Certainly, we could select some grouping of 100 great books of world literature, but it would just be an assortment, not a consensus around the ideals toward which society strives.

The backlash against globalization reflects a sense of cultural dislocation. Even if people never read the Western canon, they know it existed. They know it lay at the foundation of Western society. They feel that any disrespect for it assaults their own legitimacy. Thus, the canon has become a proxy for a fight over identity. Both the traditional and the multicultural approaches focus heavily on identity—what does a good citizen look like? What are his formative experiences? What should he know? But we face other pressing issues as well: democracy, freedom, prosperity, spirituality, justice, knowledge, happiness, and so on. The Western classics have many good things to say about these issues, so do books outside that canon. We cannot find solutions as long as every discussion keeps getting dragged back to identity. We would do well to relinquish the canon—and fights over who or what it includes and excludes—so that we can make room for more creative responses to the full range of issues we face.

Furthermore, the canon imposes a more obvious limitation on readers. It consists mainly of literature in the narrow sense. The canon invites us to apply the most sophisticated reading techniques to novels, poems, and plays, maybe along with some philosophy and history. Sophisticated interpretation is what supposedly distinguishes literature and the humanities from other fields as though we read everything else just for information. When I studied the nineteenth century in college English classes, for instance, I read every important poet and novelist from Arnold to Zola. But I was not given the century's two most influential books: Charles Darwin's *Origin of Species* and Karl Marx's *Capital*; my teachers conceded them to the economics and biology departments. They did not feel compelled to teach Marx and Darwin as literature because these writers practiced science, not culture. However, *Capital* and *The Origin of Species* created revolutions precisely because they strove to explain the world as it actually is, not as it ought to be. For reading to matter again, it will have to enlarge itself to deal directly with actualities just as economics, politics, and science do.

We have reached a major inflection point in the culture of reading. Centuries-old practices that suited the literary canon have started to evolve into a new form of reading that will reinforce the pragmatic, creative approach described in the preceding chapters. This new, reader-centric form will emerge gradually through a dialogue between our reading practices and technology. Technologies and practices reinforce one another to form specific reading cultures. Where reading practices change, we can find a change in reading technology as well. The more dramatic the change in one, the more dramatic the change in the other. Digital technology has sparked a revolution in reading such as we have not seen since the invention of moveable type in the fifteenth century and probably not since the invention of the codex book 2,000 years ago. Some of the most fundamental aspects of reading will change. By the end of this transformation, reading will look different from the form we grew up with, whose features seem eternal and unquestionable to us.

We can more clearly see the shift in reading culture that's under way if we step back and take an historical view. Books took the form of scrolls in classical antiquity. Scrolls consisted of long horizontal sheets of papyrus paper, with each end attached to a wooden rod. The lines of the text would be written in a series of vertical columns similar to our pages today. The reader would hold a rod in each hand. With one hand, he would unroll the scroll from the rod on one side to reveal the columns of text, one by one. At the same time, he would take up the scroll that he had finished reading by using the other hand to roll it onto the rod on the other side. When he finished reading, he would store the scroll in a wooden box for protection. Scrolls varied widely in length—some the equivalent of just a few pages and others dozens of pages long. A scroll would typically hold the same amount of text as a chapter in a modern printed volume. They corresponded to the "books" with which modern editions of classical works are divided today. If a Greek or Roman wanted to read an entire work, he would have to have as many scrolls as the number of "books" comprising the work—24 in the case of the *Iliad* and the *Odyssey*, 142 in the case of Livy's history of Rome.

This technology sounds large and awkward to a modern reader used to holding a paperback romance in one hand. Nevertheless, scrolls suited the culture of reading in antiquity. People read aloud, and reading generally occurred in company. Only a minority of wealthy people could afford to buy scrolls, which were created by hand, often by skilled craftsmen. People would typically ask an educated slave to read the text while they listened. People also read as a form of entertainment at social gatherings, where reading offered a way to share a common cultural heritage. The size of the scroll offered no disadvantage in these settings. Perhaps they even added to the ceremony of the occasion as scrolls could be ornate, with beautifully carved caps at the ends of the wooden rods and decorated boxes for storage.

The codex—the form of book we have today—originated in the first century B.C. in Italy. Romans traditionally used wooden boards covered in wax as scratch pads. They were about the size of a modern book. The Romans would etch words in the wax with a stylus, and when they were done with the text and needed to write something else, they would scrape the wax smooth and pick up the stylus again. Someone got the idea of tying a stack of these wooden tablets together to create a *pugiles* (from the Latin word for fist). The *pugiles*, or notebook, proved convenient, say, for the overseers of large estates who had to keep track of a lot of information about slaves, crops, and livestock. It wouldn't all fit on one wax tablet, so binding several tablets together at the edges, enabling a reader to flip through them, allowed the over-seer to carry his notes around as he toured farms. People recognized the utility of the form and, in the first century A.D., started to bind *pugiles*-size sheets of papyrus together to create the first codices.

The codex did not displace the scroll right away. The hesitation wasn't stubborn adherence to tradition in the face of a new-fangled de-vice. The scroll nicely fitted the cultural function of reading in classical antiquity, so people continued to use that format.

The codex gained ground only as another reading practice emerged. Silent reading developed among actors rehearsing their parts in dramas at Athens in late fifth century B.C. But it remained a niche practice for many centuries. It became more prevalent when Christians, who had modest means, started reading for devotion by themselves in private chambers. Silent reading allowed a Christian to contemplate God and meditate on his own sinfulness. It suited the inwardness of Christianity. The compactness of the codex permitted a believer to keep the Bible and other devotional works with him in the small spaces of ordinary houses. The spread of the codex matched the growth of Christianity. The codex didn't overtake scrolls until about 400 A.D. Even then, scrolls continued in widespread use for over 1,000 years more.

Thus, we still use the form of the book that ancient Romans and Christians invented 2,000 years ago. Of course, we use moveable type rather than hand lettering, and machines produce the pages and bind-ing rather than manual labor. Still, our books stack pages between boards in a compact format. Similarly, our reading practices stem from Christian devotional reading. For us, reading is a private pastime. We generally go off by ourselves to read or create quiet for ourselves when we cannot be alone—for example, with sound-dampening head phones on a train or plane. Reading is personal. Mostly, we choose books for our individual enjoyment or advancement. We share books with friends who like to read, too, but we seldom read aloud to others and then mostly in the privacy of the home.

Similarly, technology will influence though not determine the reading culture to come. E-books offer several advantages. They are easy to download, and they cost less than print volumes. An e-reader, smartphone, or other device can store a large number of books. We can take e-books anywhere we take those devices, including places where printed volumes would be awkward to carry. Publishers like the idea of e-books because they save printing and distribution costs and have a higher profit margin than print. For these reasons, some predicted e-books would quickly make print obsolete. In fact, e-books saw rapid growth for many years after they were introduced, but then sales declined. At the moment, they account for 15–20% of book sales. Hard covers and paperbacks still make up two thirds of book sales. The logic of technology cannot change reading culture faster than readers allow.

Up to now, e-books have been mostly electronic facsimiles of print books, which, nevertheless, omit many of the features that turn reading into a pleasure for the senses. We like having print books in our hands. We like the weight and warmth of them. We like seeing all the pleasure that awaits us embodied in a stack of pages. We like turning the pages one by one. We like the permanence of physical books. We like them as aesthetic objects. We display them. They become familiar decorations in our physical environment. When we visit others, their books draw our eye. With an e-book, a page of text appears on the screen as if from nowhere and then disappears as though it had never existed. An e-reader or smartphone is cold, hard, and unvarying. The fast pace of the digital world clashes with the slow, meditative culture of book reading. Such reading habits change slowly. A friend who plays audio books in the car tells me she pictures the text on the page as the speaker reads it rather than listening to it like music. Thus, the ingrained habit of reading physical books overrides the new format. For e-books to triumph, they will need to develop features that print books lack and that deliver a more compelling experience.

The transformation of reading culture will accelerate when technology amplifies changes already occurring in our reading practices. As noted above, reading is becoming a more social activity, with the mushrooming of book clubs and other initiatives for readers to engage one another. In the analog world, forming a community takes some work. Usually, a strong personality or a small group of friends supplies the energy, and success depends on their finding enough like-minded people among their personal acquaintance who are willing to read the monthly book and come to the meetings. Digital technology makes it much easier to build communities. Social media develop and sustain a wider circle of friends than face-to-face networking. People exchange information more easily. People can find each other based on similar interests rather than the vagaries of location and personal acquaintance. Some book clubs are even international. The activities of the book club, including meetings, can occur partly or even wholly online. Social networks can sustain the club in between meetings.

In this way, reading will become one facet of all that happens via social media. Book clubs will not differ in kind from other online activities. The same people who meet to discuss books about a shared interest in a particular issue can also organize to address that issue.

Reading will more easily lead to action. These days, social activism spreads online before it hits the streets, and social networks of readers will feed into it.

With further development, digital text can make reading still more social. For example, digital text can incorporate intertextuality into the book itself. We know that every text refers to, and depends upon, other texts, but each print book is discrete. Thus, if we want to do something as simple as look up a word, we have to get up from our chair, go to the bookshelf, find a dictionary, and thumb through it till we find the right entry. Nothing helps readers with literary references between texts; readers must be aware of the references and go looking for the original source. Readers who lack this awareness miss the references and a whole layer of meaning. Readers must lend the physical volume if they want to share a book with others and find other media for discussing the book with friends. Software tools such as Noet embed glossaries in e-books, point back to the original languages of translations, allow readers to compare texts side by side, enable a reader to annotate the text, allow sharing of insights with a social network, and provide other features that make intertextuality an organic part of the book and an easier part of reading.

Digital text will also make reading more social by offering an alternative to the permanence of the text. Since reading began 5,000 years ago, the text has always remained permanent. It is the same today as it was yesterday. It is the same for you as it is for me. But digital text can change in response to a changing context. For example, the text can be coded to disappear as soon as we read it so that it takes on the fleeting quality of a memory rather than the permanence of a monument. Or the author can place multiple hyperlinks on each page so that the reader must click on one to continue reading. By making simple choices, different readers can find different paths through the same text. The book thus offers a unique experience for each reader, who takes the art of "writing" the book at least partly into his own hands. Or books could be designed so that they can only be read by two or more people working together. In other words, books could become more like online games where players work through scenarios together. With these options made possible by digital text, readers would each find something different in every book so that they would seek out others to share their discoveries and to learn new ways to get more out of the experience.

Creativity and community will increasingly drive reading while the influence of the literary canon fades. The canon has become a hollow form, reverenced for its past associations yet less and less relevant to our lives. The cultural context in which the canon played a vital role has changed, and nostalgia for the canon will not restore its vitality. We will find more value in books if we stop relying on authorities to tell us what to read and how to think about books. Instead, we should rely on ourselves and each other to derive insights from reading and apply them to the problems we face today.

If I had been quick-witted, I would have recommended that my dental hygienist take advice about reading from Vergil. In *The Divine Comedy*, Vergil serves as Dante's guide through hell and purgatory. Vergil represents the wisdom and learning of classical antiquity. *The Divine Comedy* is really a tour through all the books Dante has read. But as a pagan, Vergil cannot enter heaven. In Canto XXVII of the *Purgatorio*, Dante and Vergil reach the top of Mt. Purgatory and pause at the entrance to the garden of the Earthly Paradise, the antechamber of heaven. Vergil reveals that he can accompany Dante no farther and offers this parting guidance:

> I've brought you here through intellect and art;
> from now on, let your pleasure be your guide ...[5]
> (Purgatorio, Canto xxvii, ll. 130–131)

In other words, at some point, the skills and knowledge we gain as educated readers fail us. We confront an environment that they have not prepared us for. We must draw on other abilities—our sense of pleasure, our intuition, our imagination—in order to find our way. We readers now pause at the entrance to a new culture of reading whose riches we can barely conceive. As we move forward, we will make discoveries not of things that are already known to others but of things that are yet unknown. We enter the realm of the unknown. The rules change. We can only open ourselves wide to the possibilities that will emerge.

The pleasure that Vergil mentions requires as much discipline in its way as critical reading does. Or maybe nerve is a better term. We have to trust our own appetites for reading rather than follow some external notion of what to read. Those appetites look shallow or arbitrary in the moment. Why do we like anything? Desire is irrational and easy to dismiss. When I was a teenager I binged on Agatha Christie, Dorothy Sayers, and Ian Fleming, often when I should have done schoolwork. I rushed home from school one day because I was dying to finish Sayers' *Murder Must Advertise*. I've never been more enthralled by a book than during the climactic cricket scene. At the time, this sort of reading felt like mere entertainment. I see the value to me more now in retrospect. Without realizing it, I learned about the power of careful word choice and structure to lead readers in a certain direction. I learned basics of writing, such as plot, dialogue, characterization, and setting. By slurping up those books for pleasure, I gained a more instinctive understanding of these things than if I had studied them formally.

More importantly, indulging one appetite leads us to discover other appetites. Christie and Sayers had read the classics—Dickens, Shakespeare, Dante, and so on—and they incorporated bits and pieces into their mysteries. Sayers made Abbé Prévost's novel *Manon Lescaut* into a clue in *Clouds of Witness*. When I happened across *Manon Lescaut* in a bookstore, I bought it and read it. I might never have done so otherwise. So mysteries and thrillers whetted my appetite for certain other kinds of literature, and from there I continued on to still other kinds of books and the discoveries I made in them. All of these negligible little steps, taken under the impulse of immediate desire, over time filled out the profile of a life that is uniquely mine.

We must assess our own desires when we let pleasure be our guide, and that is hard to do. We must distinguish between the desire of the heart and the coaxing of vanity. Does the soul drive us to read those books, or do we merely want to think of ourselves as the kind of people who have read them? Perhaps my dental hygienist fell into the latter category. If she had felt the need to read the classics from her soul, she would have read them without encouragement from anyone else. We struggle to discern which impulse to obey, especially when others recommend books to us. Sometimes we look for new reading experiences. We want books that we wouldn't have found on our own. Recommendations take us to places we could not have foreseen. At other times, we need particular food. But most people recommend books that they themselves liked or that they happened to hear about; they do not make the recommendation out of careful consideration for our needs. It's a rare friend who does so. As with *Manon Lescaut*, references to other works in a book that we have read and liked are more reliable. We developed intimacy with the book, so it knows our soul and what it seeks.

The soul is the irreducible element of meaning. We cannot find meaning in a book or share it with others unless it has first sunk deep into our own soul. Humans possess an instinct for meaning if they have the nerve to follow out the pleasure of it. Readers have long been taught that writers possess this instinct. Now, with traditional institutions decaying, readers have little choice but to trust themselves. Fortunately, technology will give readers greater support than they have ever had before in improvising their own path.

NOTES

1 Terry Eagleton, *Literary Theory: An Introduction* (Minneapolis: University of Minnesota Press, 1984), p. 24ff.
2 Matthew Arnold, *Poetry and Criticism of Matthew Arnold*, ed. A. Dwight Culler (Boston: Houghton Mifflin Company, 1961), p. 411.
3 Ibid., p. 409.
4 George Will, "Literary Politics," *Newsweek* (22 April, 1991).
5 Dante Alighieri, *The Divine Comedy*, vol. II *Purgatorio*, tr. Allen Mandelbaum (New York: Bantam Books, 1982), p. 255.

Index

These critical terms appear throughout *The Future of Reading* and therefore are omitted from the index: book, meaning, reader/reading, text, writer/writing, word, world.

Dodds, E.R. 59, 61–2, 64–5, 73; *The Greeks and the Irrational* 59, 61
Dostoevsky, Fyodor 80, 146; *The Idiot* 80–1
drama 10, 42, 44–5, 51, 53, 62, 64, 66–7, 73, 150–1, 166
dreams, dreaming 7, 20–1, 26, 28–31, 33, 37–8, 40, 66, 82, 85, 93, 103–4, 119, 121, 144, 149, 151
duration block *see* time

economics, economists x, 3, 46, 72, 141–2, 144–8, 153–5, 161, 164
education 70, 106, 111, 134, 141, 148, 160, 162–3, 165, 169
ego 36–8, 85, 87, 94
Eliot, George 37
Eliot, T.S. 148
Emerson, Ralph Waldo 22–30
emotion *see* feelings
empathy 80, 90, 158
empiricism 29, 38, 54
enactment 13, 22, 40, 51–2, 110, 115
Engels, Friedrich 14
English 26, 57, 83, 86, 118–21, 161
epic 53, 56, 71, 89, 102, 123–4, 147, 151
ethics *see* morality
Euripides 59–65, 149–50; *Alcestis* 62; *The Bacchae* 59–65, 75, 150
event 6, 9, 44, 48, 62, 70, 80, 101
evidence 46, 62, 65, 82
experience ix, 2, 7, 12, 20–4, 27, 29, 33, 35–6, 38, 40, 42, 46, 51, 55–7, 65–7, 70–5, 79–80, 84–6, 89–90, 111, 117–18, 120, 122, 130, 137–40, 142, 144–5, 151, 156, 159, 164, 167–8, 170
experiment 13–14, 69, 71, 73, 101, 109, 132, 136–7, 139, 146, 151, 154
expertise, experts 3–4, 6–7, 134

fact 12, 23, 44, 63, 85, 87, 117, 130, 133–4, 138, 143, 152
faculties 10, 22, 49, 52–4, 65, 80–1, 90
fantasy 53, 131, 133, 146

fate 39–40, 49, 98, 111
fear 5, 10, 21, 35, 62, 80, 84–6, 96, 120
feelings 2, 20–2, 29–30, 35, 38–9, 46, 48, 52, 54, 65, 71, 73–5, 80–1, 85, 87, 90, 92–4, 104–5, 121–2, 130, 133–4, 138–1, 154, 156
feminism 46, 65
fiction *see* novels
field *see* discipline
Flaubert, Gustav 82; *Trois Contes* 82
Fleming, Ian 43, 169
framework *see* model
freedom 1–2, 7, 9, 11, 31, 52, 72, 75, 86, 114, 141, 164
French 82–3
Freud, Sigmund 33–4, 37
friction *see* resistance
future 6, 25, 40, 100–1

García Márquez, Gabriel 86; *One Hundred Years of Solitude* 86–7
Garland, Hamlin 82; *Main Traveled Roads* 82
German 118, 132
Gilgamesh 151–2
God, gods 4–5, 22, 39–40, 42–3, 47–8, 50–1, 59–64, 66–7, 70, 87, 90, 95–8, 100–4, 106–7, 110–13, 134, 139–40, 151, 161, 166; Apollo 62, 67, 98, 150; Chronos 102; Demeter 67; Dionysos 59–64, 149–50; Egeria 97; Hermes 82; Jesus 68, 112; Jove/Zeus 98, 107; Memory 102; muse 100–4, 106–8; Ouranos 102; Shamash 110; Tritogeneia 98; Venus 4–5
Goethe, Johann Wolfgang von 162; *Wilhelm Meister's Apprenticeship* 162
government 6, 13, 58, 60, 96, 111, 141, 147
grammar *see* syntax
Greece, Greeks 9, 38–40, 59–61, 65, 70, 98–9, 102, 104, 111, 118, 134–5, 165
Greek 118, 133–4, 160